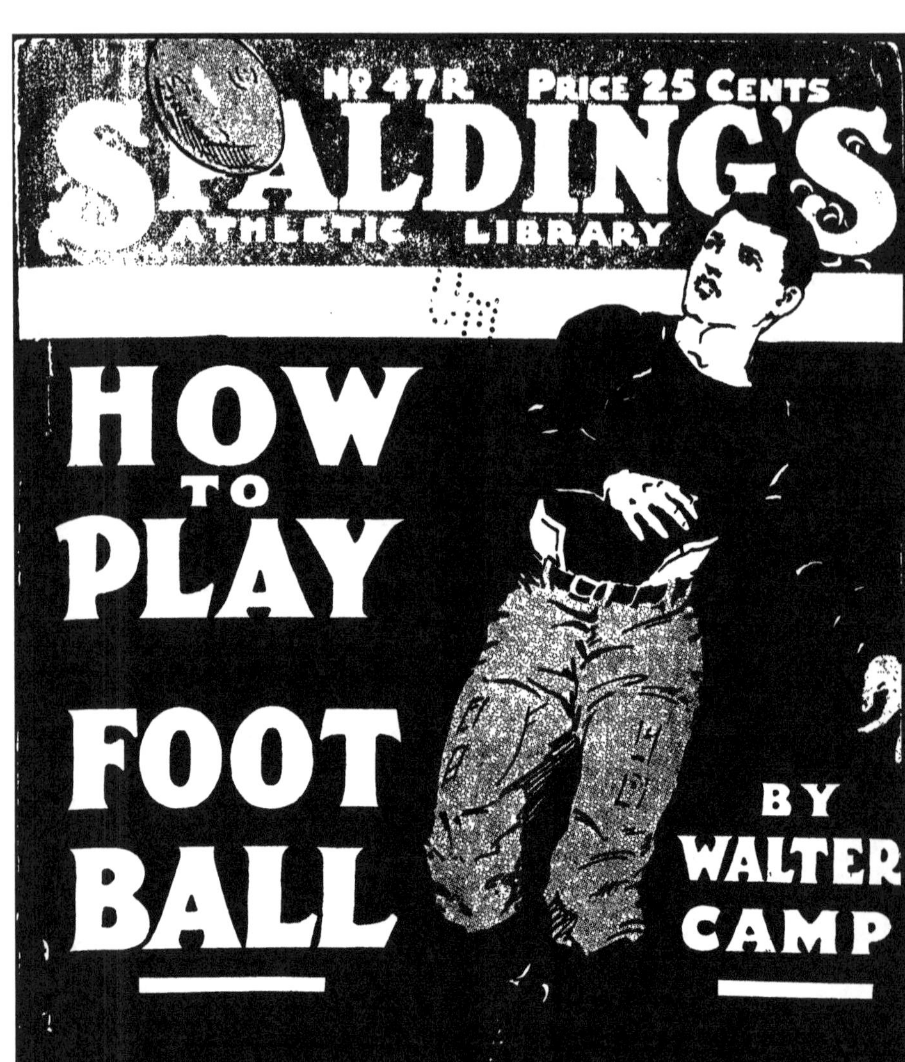
No 47R
PRICE 25 CENTS
SPALDING'S
ATHLETIC LIBRARY
HOW
TO
PLAY
FOOT
BALL
BY
WALTER
CAMP
AMERICAN SPORTS PUBLISHING Co.
21 Warren Street, New York

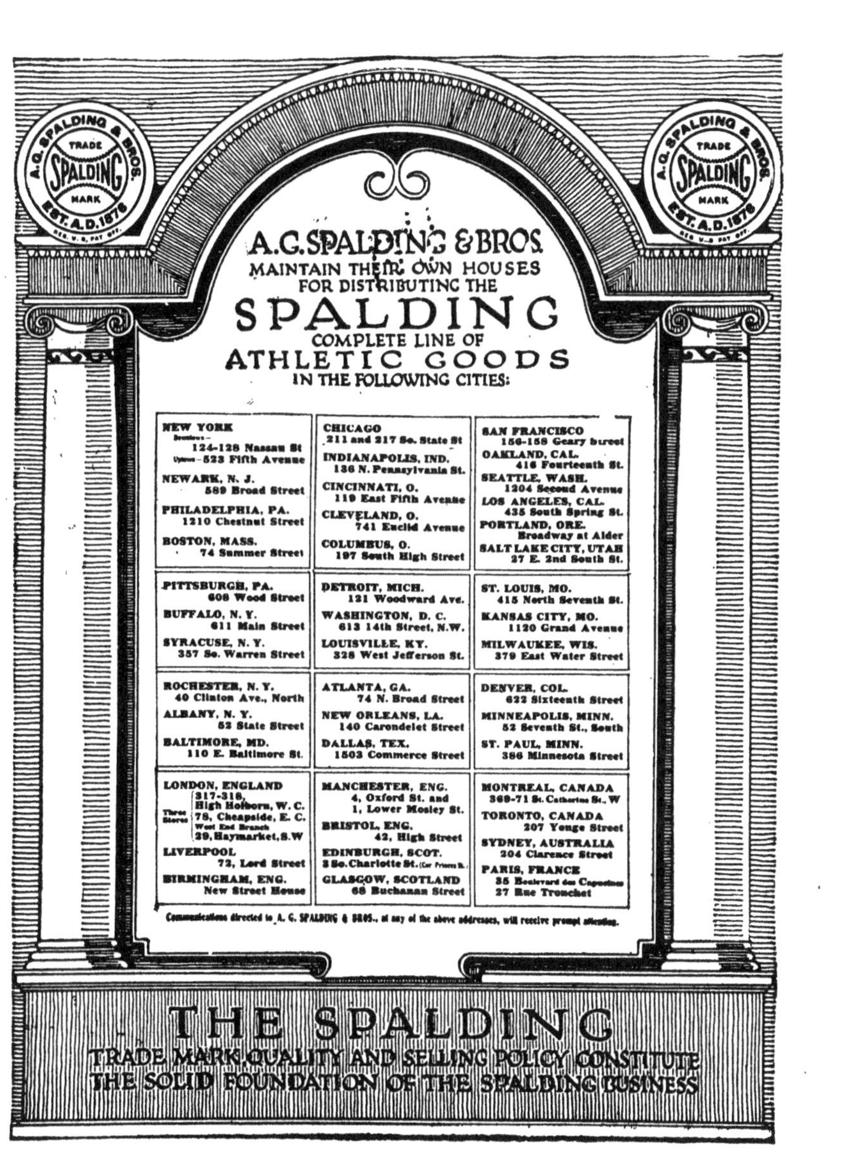

A.G. SPALDING & BROS. TRADE SPALDING MARK EST. A.D. 1876
A.G. SPALDING & BROS.
MAINTAIN THEIR OWN HOUSES
FOR DISTRIBUTING THE
SPALDING
COMPLETE LINE OF
ATHLETIC GOODS
IN THE FOLLOWING CITIES:
NEW YORK
Downtown – 124-128 Nassau St
Uptown – 523 Fifth Avenue
NEWARK, N. J.
589 Broad Street
PHILADELPHIA, PA.
1210 Chestnut Street
BOSTON, MASS.
74 Summer Street
CHICAGO
211 and 217 So. State St
INDIANAPOLIS, IND.
136 N. Pennsylvania St.
CINCINNATI, O.
119 East Fifth Avenue
CLEVELAND, O.
741 Euclid Avenue
COLUMBUS, O.
197 South High Street
SAN FRANCISCO
156-158 Geary Street
OAKLAND, CAL.
416 Fourteenth St.
SEATTLE, WASH.
1204 Second Avenue
LOS ANGELES, CAL.
435 South Spring St.
PORTLAND, ORE.
Broadway at Alder
SALT LAKE CITY, UTAH
27 E. 2nd South St.
PITTSBURGH, PA.
608 Wood Street
BUFFALO, N. Y.
611 Main Street
SYRACUSE, N. Y.
357 So. Warren Street
DETROIT, MICH.
121 Woodward Ave.
WASHINGTON, D. C.
613 14th Street, N.W.
LOUISVILLE, KY.
328 West Jefferson St.
ST. LOUIS, MO.
415 North Seventh St.
KANSAS CITY, MO.
1120 Grand Avenue
MILWAUKEE, WIS.
379 East Water Street
ROCHESTER, N. Y.
40 Clinton Ave., North
ALBANY, N. Y.
52 State Street
BALTIMORE, MD.
110 E. Baltimore St.
ATLANTA, GA.
74 N. Broad Street
NEW ORLEANS, LA.
140 Carondelet Street
DALLAS, TEX.
1503 Commerce Street
DENVER, COL.
622 Sixteenth Street
MINNEAPOLIS, MINN.
52 Seventh St., South
ST. PAUL, MINN.
386 Minnesota Street
LONDON, ENGLAND
Three Stores
317-318, High Holborn, W. C.
78, Cheapside, E. C.
West End Branch
29, Haymarket, S.W
LIVERPOOL
72, Lord Street
BIRMINGHAM, ENG.
New Street House
MANCHESTER, ENG.
4, Oxford St. and
1, Lower Mosley St.
BRISTOL, ENG.
42, High Street
EDINBURGH, SCOT.
3 So. Charlotte St. (Cor Princes St.)
GLASGOW, SCOTLAND
68 Buchanan Street
MONTREAL, CANADA
369-71 St. Catherine St., W
TORONTO, CANADA
207 Yonge Street
SYDNEY, AUSTRALIA
204 Clarence Street
PARIS, FRANCE
35 Boulevard des Capucines
27 Rue Tronchet
Communications directed to A. G. SPALDING & BROS., at any of the above addresses, will receive prompt attention.
THE SPALDING
TRADE MARK QUALITY AND SELLING POLICY CONSTITUTE
THE SOLID FOUNDATION OF THE SPALDING BUSINESS

SPALDING ATHLETIC LIBRARY

SPALDING OFFICIAL ANNUALS

No. 1. SPALDING'S OFFICIAL BASE BALL GUIDE. . . . . Price 10c.
No. 1S. SPALDING'S OFFICIAL BASE BALL GUIDE. (Spanish Edition) . Price 10c.
No. 2. SPALDING'S OFFICIAL FOOT BALL GUIDE. . . . . Price 10c.
No. 6. SPALDING'S OFFICIAL ICE HOCKEY GUIDE. . . . . Price 10c.
No. 7. SPALDING'S OFFICIAL BASKET BALL GUIDE. . . . Price 10c.
No. 7A. SPALDING'S OFFICIAL WOMEN'S BASKET BALL GUIDE. Price 10c.
No. 9. SPALDING'S OFFICIAL INDOOR BASE BALL GUIDE. . Price 10c.
No. 12A. SPALDING'S OFFICIAL ATHLETIC RULES. . . Price 10c.
No. 1R. SPALDING'S OFFICIAL ATHLETIC ALMANAC. . . Price 25c.
No. 3R. SPALDING'S OFFICIAL GOLF GUIDE. . . . Price 25c.
No. 55R. SPALDING'S OFFICIAL SOCCER FOOT BALL GUIDE. . Price 25c.
No. 57R. SPALDING'S LAWN TENNIS ANNUAL. . . . . Price 25c.
No. 59R. SPALDING'S OFFICIAL BASE BALL RECORD. . . . Price 25c.

Specially Bound Series of Athletic Handbooks

Flexible binding. Mailed postpaid on receipt of 50 cents each number.

No. 501L. STROKES AND SCIENCE OF LAWN TENNIS
No. 502L. HOW TO PLAY GOLF
No. 503L. HOW TO PLAY FOOT BALL
No. 504L. ART OF SKATING
No. 505L. GET WELL—KEEP WELL
No. 506L. HOW TO LIVE 100 YEARS
No. 507L. HOW TO WRESTLE
No. 508L. HOW TO PLAY LAWN TENNIS; HOW TO PLAY TENNIS FOR BEGINNERS
No. 509L. BOXING
No. 510L. DUMB BELL EXERCISES
No. 511L. JIU JITSU
No. 512L. SPEED SWIMMING
No. 513L. WINTER SPORTS
No. 514L. HOW TO BOWL
No. 515L. HOW TO SWIM AND COMPETITIVE DIVING.
No. 516L. SCHOOL TACTICS AND MAZE RUNNING; CHILDREN'S GAMES.
No. 517L. TEN AND TWENTY MINUTE EXERCISES
No. 518L. INDOOR AND OUTDOOR GYMNASTIC GAMES
No. 519L. SPALDING'S OFFICIAL BASE BALL GUIDE
No. 520L. SPALDING'S OFFICIAL FOOT BALL GUIDE
No. 521L. SPALDING'S OFFICIAL BASKET BALL GUIDE
No. 522L. GOLF FOR GIRLS
No. 523L. HOW TO PLAY BASE BALL; HOW TO UMPIRE; HOW TO MANAGE A TEAM, ETC.
No. 524L. SPALDING'S LAWN TENNIS ANNUAL
No. 525L. HOW TO PITCH; READY RECKONER OF BASE BALL PERCENTAGES
No. 526L. HOW TO CATCH; HOW TO BAT

In addition to above, any 25 cent "Red Cover" book listed in Spalding's Athletic Library will be bound in flexible binding for 50 cents each; or any two 10 cent "Green Cover" or "Blue Cover" books in one volume for 50 cents.

(Continued on the next page.)

ANY OF THE ABOVE BOOKS MAILED POSTPAID UPON RECEIPT OF PRICE

5-1-17

SPALDING ATHLETIC LIBRARY

Group I. Base Ball

"Blue Cover" Series, each number 10c.

No. 1 Spalding's Official Base Ball Guide
No. 1S Spalding's Official Base Ball Guide. Spanish Edition.
No. 202 How to Play Base Ball
No. 219 Ready Reckoner of Base Ball [Percentages
No. 223 How to Bat
No. 224 How to Play the Outfield
No. 225 How to Play First Base
No. 226 How to Play Second Base
No. 227 How to Play Third Base
No. 228 How to Play Shortstop
No. 229 How to Catch
No. 230 How to Pitch
No. 231 { How to Organize a Base Ball League [Club
How to Organize a Base Ball
How to Manage a Base Ball Club
How to Train a Base Ball Team
How to Captain a Base Ball Team
Technical Base Ball Terms }
No. 232 How to Run Bases
No. 350 How to Score
No. 355 Minor League Base Ball Guide
No. 356 Official Book National League of Prof. Base Ball Clubs
No. 9 Spalding's Official Indoor Base Ball Guide

"Red Cover" Series, each number 25c.

No. 59R. Official Base Ball Record
No. 75R. How to Umpire

Group II. Foot Ball

"Blue Cover" Series, each number 10c.

No. 2 Spalding's Official Foot Ball Guide
No. 358 Official College Soccer Guide

"Red Cover" Series, each number 25c.

No. 39R. How to Play Soccer
No. 47R. How to Play Foot Ball
No. 55R. Spalding's Official Soccer Foot Ball Guide

Group III. Tennis

"Blue Cover" Series, each number 10c.

No. 157 How to Play Lawn Tennis
No. 363 Tennis Errors and Remedies

"Green Cover" Series, each number 10c.

No. 1P. How to Play Tennis—For Beginners. By P. A. Vaile

"Red Cover" Series, each number 25c.

No. 2R. Strokes and Science of Lawn Tennis [tralasia
No. 42R. Davis Cup Contests in Aus-
No. 57R. Spalding's Lawn Tennis
No. 76R. Tennis for Girls [Annual

Group IV. Golf

"Green Cover" Series, each number 10c.

No. 2P. How to Learn Golf

"Red Cover" Series, each number 25c

No. 3R. Spalding's Official Gol
No. 4R. How to Play Golf [Guid
No. 63R. Golf for Girls

Group V. Basket Ball

"Blue Cover" Series, each number 10c.

No. 7 Spalding's Official Basket Ball Guide
No. 7A Spalding's Official Women's Basket Ball Guide
No. 193 How to Play Basket Ball

Group VI. Skating and Winter Sports

"Blue Cover" Series, each number 10c.

No. 6 Spalding's Official Ice Hockey
No. 14 Curling [Guide

"Red Cover" Series, each number 25c.

No. 8R. The Art of Skating
No. 20R. How to Play Ice Hockey
No. 28R. Winter Sports
No. 72R. Figure Skating for Women

Group VII. Field and Track Athletics

"Blue Cover" Series, each number 10c.

No. 12A Spalding's Official Athletic Rules
No. 27 College Athletics
No. 55 Official Sporting Rules
No. 87 Athletic Primer
No. 156 Athletes' Guide
No. 178 How to Train for Bicycling
No. 182 All Around Athletics
No. 255 How to Run 100 Yards
No. 302 Y. M. C. A. Official Handbook
No. 317 Marathon Running
No. 342 Walking for Health and Competition
No. 362 Track, Relay and Cross Country Rules of the National Collegiate Athletic Ass'n.

"Green Cover" Series, each number 10c.

No. 3P. How to Become an Athlete By James E. Sullivan
No. 4P. How to Sprint

"Red Cover" Series, each number 25c.

No. 1R. Spalding's Official Athletic Almanac
No. 17R. Olympic Games, Stockholm, 1912 [book
No. 45R. Intercollegiate Official Hand-
No. 48R. Distance and Cross Country Running
No. 70R. How to Become a Weight Thrower

(Continued on the next page.)

ANY OF THE ABOVE BOOKS MAILED POSTPAID UPON RECEIPT OF PRICE

SPALDING ATHLETIC LIBRARY

Group VIII. School Athletics

"Blue Cover" Series, each number 10c.

No. 246 Athletic Training for Schoolboys

"Red Cover" Series, each number 25c.

No. 61R. School Tactics and Maze Running; Children's Games
No. 66R. Calisthenic Drills and Fancy Marching and Physical Training for the School and Class Room
No. 71R. Public Schools Athletic League Official Handbook
No. 74R. Schoolyard Athletics

Group IX. Water Sports

"Blue Cover" Series, each number 10c.

No. 128 How to Row
No. 129 Water Polo
No. 361 Intercollegiate Swimming [Guide

"Red Cover" Series, each number 25c.

No. 36R. Speed Swimming
No. 37R. How to Swim
No. 60R. Canoeing and Camping

Group X. Athletic Games for Women and Girls

"Blue Cover" Series, each number 10c.

No. 7A Spalding's Official Women's Basket Ball Guide
No. 314 Girls' Athletics

"Red Cover" Series, each number 25c.

No. 38R. Field Hockey
No. 41R. Newcomb
No. 63R. Golf for Girls
No. 69R. Girls and Athletics

Group XI. Lawn and Field Games

"Blue Cover" Series, each number 10c.

No. 167 Quoits
No. 170 Push Ball
No. 180 Ring Hockey
No. 199 Equestrian Polo
No. 201 How to Play Lacrosse
No. 207 Lawn Bowls

"Red Cover" Series, each number, 25c.

No. 6R. Cricket, and How to Play It

Group XII. Miscellaneous Games

"Blue Cover" Series, each number 10c.

No. 13 American Game of Hand Ball
No. 364 Volley Ball

"Red Cover" Series, each number 25c.

No. 43R. Archery, Roque, Croquet, English Croquet, Lawn Hockey, Tether Ball, Clock Golf, Golf-Croquet, Hand Tennis, Hand Polo, Wicket Polo, Badminton, Drawing Room Hockey, Garden Hockey, Basket Goal, Volley Ball Rules and Pin Ball
No. 49R. How to Bowl
No. 50R. Court Games

Group XIII. Manly Sports

"Blue Cover" Series, each number 10c.

No. 191 How to Punch the Bag
No. 282 Roller Skating Guide

"Red Cover" Series, each number 25c.

No. 11R. Fencing Foil Work Illustrat[ed
No. 19R. Professional Wrestling
No. 21R. Jiu Jitsu
No. 25R. Boxing
No. 30R. The Art of Fencing
No. 65R. How to Wrestle

Group XIV. Calisthenics

"Red Cover" Series, each number 25c.

No. 10R. Single Stick Drill
No. 16R. Team Wand Drill
No. 22R. Indian Clubs and Dumb Bells and Pulley Weights
No. 24R. Dumb Bell Exercises
No. 73R. Graded Calisthenics and Dumb Bell Drills

Group XV. Gymnastics

"Blue Cover" Series, each number 10c.

No. 124 How to Become a Gymnast
No. 254 Barnjum Bar Bell Drill
No. 287 Fancy Dumb Bell and Marching Drills

"Red Cover" Series, each number 25c.

No. 14R. Trapeze, Long Horse and Rope Exercises
No. 34R. Grading of Gym. Exercises
No. 40R. Indoor and Outdoor Gymnastic Games
No. 52R. Pyramid Building
No. 56R. Tumbling for Amateurs and Ground Tumbling
No. 67R. Exercises on the Side Horse: Exercises on the Flying Rings.
No. 68R. Horizontal Bar Exercises; Exercises on Parallel Bars

Group XVI. Home Exercising

"Blue Cover" Series, each number 10c.

No. 161 Ten Minutes' Exercise for [Busy Men
No. 185 Hints on Health
No. 325 Twenty-Minute Exercises

"Red Cover" Series, each number 25c

No. 7R. Physical Training Simplified
No. 9R. How to Live 100 Years
No. 23R. Get Well; Keep Well
No. 33R. Tensing Exercises
No. 51R. 285 Health Answers
No. 54R. Medicine Ball Exercises, Indigestion Treated by Gymnastics, Physical Education and Hygiene
No. 62R. The Care of the Body
No. 64R. Muscle Building; Health by Muscular Gymnastics

ANY OF THE ABOVE BOOKS MAILED POSTPAID UPON RECEIPT OF PRICE

5-1-17

WALTER CAMP
YALE
MEMBER RULES COMMITTEE.

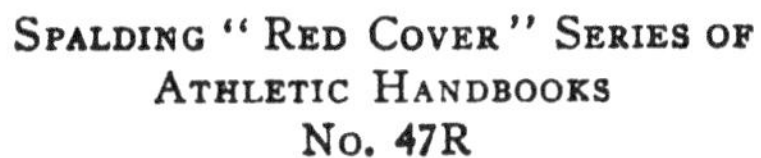

Spalding "Red Cover" Series of
Athletic Handbooks
No. 47R

How to Play Foot Ball

A Primer on the Modern College Game with Tactics Brought Down to Date

EDITED BY
WALTER CAMP

PUBLISHED BY
AMERICAN SPORTS PUBLISHING COMPANY
21 Warren Street, New York

Contents

All-America Teams Since 1889

SELECTED BY WALTER CAMP.

	1889	1890	1891
End	Cumnock, Harvard.	Hallowell, Harvard.	Hinkey, Yale.
Tackle	Cowan, Princeton.	Newell, Harvard.	Winter, Yale.
Guard	Cranston, Harvard.	Riggs, Princeton.	Heffelfinger, Yale.
Center	George, Princeton.	Cranston, Harvard.	Adams, Pennsylvania.
Guard	Heffelfinger, Yale.	Heffelfinger, Yale.	Riggs, Princeton.
Tackle	Gill, Yale.	Rhodes, Yale.	Newell, Harvard.
End	Stagg, Yale.	Warren, Princeton.	Hartwell, Yale.
Quarter	Poe, Princeton.	Dean, Harvard.	King, Princeton.
Half	Lee, Harvard.	Corbett, Harvard.	Lake, Harvard.
Half	Channing, Princeton.	McClung, Yale.	McClung, Yale.
Full	Ames, Princeton.	Homans, Princeton.	Homans, Princeton.

	1892	1893	1894
End	Hinkey, Yale.	Hinkey, Yale.	Hinkey, Yale.
Tackle	Wallis, Yale.	Lea, Princeton.	Waters, Harvard.
Guard	Waters, Harvard.	Wheeler, Princeton.	Wheeler, Princeton.
Center	Lewis, Harvard.	Lewis, Harvard.	Stillman, Yale.
Guard	Wheeler, Princeton.	Hickok, Yale.	Hickok, Yale.
Tackle	Newell, Harvard.	Newell, Harvard.	Lea, Princeton.
End	Hallowell, Harvard.	Trenchard, Princeton.	Gelbert, Pennsylvania.
Quarter	McCormick, Yale.	King, Princeton.	Adee, Yale.
Half	Brewer, Harvard.	Brewer, Harvard.	Knipe, Pennsylvania.
Half	King, Princeton.	Morse, Princeton.	Brooke, Pennsylvania.
Full	Thayer, Pennsylvania.	Butterworth, Yale.	Butterworth, Yale.

	1895	1896	1897
End	Cabot, Harvard.	Cabot, Harvard.	Cochran, Princeton.
Tackle	Lea, Princeton.	Church, Princeton.	Chamberlain, Yale.
Guard	Wharton, Pennsylvania.	Wharton, Pennsylvania.	Hare, Pennsylvania.
Center	Bull, Pennsylvanfa.	Gailey, Princeton.	Doucette, Harvard.
Guard	Riggs, Princeton.	Woodruff, Pennsylvania.	Brown, Yale.
Tackle	Murphy, Yale.	Murphy, Yale.	Outland, Pennsylvania.
End	Gelbert, Pennsylvania.	Gelbert, Pennsylvania.	Hall, Yale.
Quarter	Wyckoff, Cornell.	Fincke, Yale.	DeSaulles, Yale.
Half	Thorne, Yale.	Wrightington, Harvard.	Dibblee, Harvard.
Half	Brewer, Harvard.	Kelly, Princeton.	Kelly, Princeton.
Full	Brooke, Pennsylvania.	Baird, Princeton.	Minds, Pennsylvania.

	1898	1899	1900
End	Palmer, Princeton.	Campbell, Harvard.	Campbell, Harvard.
Tackle	Hillebrand, Princeton.	Hillebrand, Princeton.	Bloomer, Yale.
Guard	Hare, Pennsylvania.	Hare, Pennsylvania.	Brown, Yale.
Center	Overfield, Pennsylvania.	Overfield, Pennsylvania.	Olcott, Yale.
Guard	Brown, Yale.	Brown, Yale.	Hare, Pennsylvania.
Tackle	Chamberlain, Yale.	Stillman, Yale.	Stillman, Yale.
End	Hallowell, Harvard.	Poe, Princeton.	Hallowell, Harvard.
Quarter	Daly, Harvard.	Daly, Harvard.	Fincke, Yale.
Half	Outland, Pennsylvania.	Seneca, Indians.	Chadwick, Yale.
Half	Dibblee, Harvard.	McCracken, Pennsylvania.	Morley, Columbia.
Full	Hirschberger, Chicago.	McBride, Yale.	Hale, Yale.

	1901	1902	1903.
End.........	Campbell, Harvard.	Shevlin, Yale.	Henry, Princeton.
Tackle......	Cutts, Harvard.	Hogan, Yale.	Hogan, Yale.
Guard.......	Warner, Cornell.	DeWitt, Princeton.	DeWitt, Princeton.
Center......	Holt, Yale.	Holt, Yale.	Hooper, Dartmouth.
Guard.......	Lee, Harvard.	Glass, Yale.	A. Marshall, Harvard.
Tackle......	Bunker, West Point.	Kinney, Yale.	Knowlton, Harvard.
End.........	Davis, Princeton.	Bowditch, Harvard.	Rafferty, Yale.
Quarter.....	Daly, West Point.	Rockwell, Yale.	Johnson, Carlisle.
Half........	Kernan, Harvard.	Chadwick, Yale.	Heston, Michigan.
Half........	Weekes, Columbia.	Bunker, West Point.	Kafer, Princeton.
Full.........	Graydon, Harvard.	Graydon, Harvard.	Smith, Columbia.

	1904	1905	1906
End.........	Shevlin, Yale.	Shevlin, Yale.	Forbes, Yale.
Tackle......	Cooney, Princeton.	Lamson, Pennsylvania.	Biglow, Yale.
Guard.......	Piekarski, Pennsylvania.	Tripp, Yale.	Burr, Harvard.
Center......	Tipton, West Point.	Torrey, Pennsylvania.	Dunn, Penn State.
Guard.......	Kinney, Yale.	Burr, Harvard.	Thompson, Cornell.
Tackle......	Hogan, Yale.	Squires, Harvard.	Cooney, Princeton.
End.........	Eckersall, Chicago.	Glaze, Dartmouth.	Wister, Princeton.
Quarter.....	Stevenson, Pennsylvania.	Eckersall, Chicago.	Eckersall, Chicago.
Half........	Hurley, Harvard.	Roome, Yale.	Mayhew, Brown.
Half........	Heston, Michigan.	Hubbard, Amherst.	Knox, Yale.
Full.........	Smith, Pennsylvania.	McCormick, Princeton.	Veeder, Yale.

	1907	1908	1909
End.........	Dague, Annapolis.	Scarlett, Pennsylvania.	Regnier, Brown.
Tackle......	Draper, Pennsylvania.	Fish, Harvard.	Fish, Harvard.
Guard.......	Ziegler, Pennsylvania.	Goebel, Yale.	Benbrook, Michigan.
Center......	Schulz, Michigan.	Nourse, Harvard.	Cooney, Yale.
Guard.......	Erwin, West Point.	Tobin, Dartmouth.	Andrus, Yale.
Tackle......	Biglow, Yale.	Horr, Syracuse.	Hobbs, Yale.
End.........	Alcott, Yale.	Schildmiller, Dartmouth.	Kilpatrick, Yale.
Quarter.....	Jones, Yale.	Steffen, Chicago.	McGovern, Minnesota.
Half........	Wendell, Harvard.	Tibbott, Princeton.	Philbin, Yale.
Half........	Harlan, Princeton.	Hollenbach, Pennsylvania.	Minot, Harvard.
Full.........	McCormick, Princeton.	Coy, Yale.	Coy, Yale.

	1910	1911	1912
End.........	Kilpatrick, Yale.	White, Princeton.	Felton, Harvard.
Tackle......	Walker, Minnesota.	Hart, Princeton.	Englehorn, Dartmouth.
Guard.......	Benbrook, Michigan.	Fisher, Harvard.	Pennock, Harvard.
Center......	Cozens, Pennsylvania.	Ketcham, Yale.	Ketcham, Yale.
Guard.......	Fisher, Harvard.	Duff, Princeton.	Logan, Princeton.
Tackle......	McKay, Harvard.	Devore, West Point.	Butler, Wisconsin.
End.........	Wells, Michigan.	Bomeisler, Yale.	Bomeisler, Yale.
Quarter.....	Sprackling, Brown.	Howe, Yale.	Crother, Brown.
Half........	Wendell, Harvard.	Wendell, Harvard.	Brickley, Harvard.
Half........	Pendleton, Princeton.	Thorpe, Carlisle.	Thorpe, Carlisle.
Full.........	Mercer, Pennsylvania.	Dalton, Annapolis.	Mercer, Pennsylvania.

	1913	1914	1915.
End.........	Hogsett, Dartmouth.	Hardwick, Harvard	Baston, Minnesota
Tackle......	Ballin, Princeton.	Ballin, Princeton	Gilman, Harvard
Guard.......	Pennock, Harvard.	Pennock, Harvard	Spears, Dartmouth
Center......	Des Jardien, Chicago.	McEwan, West Point	Peck, Pittsburgh
Guard.......	Brown, Navy.	Chapman, Illinois	Schlachter, Syracuse
Tackle......	Talbot, Yale.	Trumbull, Harvard	Abell, Colgate
End.........	Merillat, Army.	O'Hearn, Cornell	Shelton, Cornell
Quarter.....	Huntington, Colgate.	Ghee, Dartmouth	Barrett, Cornell
Half........	Craig, Michigan.	Maulbetsch, Michigan	King, Harvard
Half........	Brickley, Harvard.	Bradlee, Harvard	Macomber, Illinois
Full.........	Mahan, Harvard.	Mahan, Harvard	Mahan, Harvard

An Introductory Chapter for Beginners

By Walter Camp.

Those who are taking up the sport for the first time should observe certain rules which will enable them to become adept players with less mistakes than perhaps would otherwise fall to their lot.

A beginner in foot ball should do two things: He should read the rules, and he should, if possible, watch the practice. If the latter be impossible, he and his men must, after having read the rules, start in and, with eleven on a side, play according to their own interpretation of these rules. When differences of opinion arise as to the meaning of any rule, a letter addressed to the publishers of Spalding's Official Foot Ball Guide—the American Sports Publishing Company, 21 Warren Street, New York—will always elicit a ready and satisfactory answer.

The first thing to be done in starting the practice is to provide the accessories of the game, which, in foot ball, are of the simplest kind. The field should be marked out with ordinary lime lines. It is customary, though unnecessary, to mark the field with transverse lines, every five yards, for the benefit of the referee in determining how far the ball is advanced at every down. In the middle of the lines forming the ends of the field, the goal posts are erected, and should be eighteen feet six inches apart, with cross-bar ten feet from the ground. The posts should project several feet above the cross-bar. The ball used is an oval leather cover containing a rubber bladder, which is inflated by means of a small air pump. The ball used by the principal teams is the Official Intercollegiate Foot Ball, No. J5, adopted by the Intercollegiate Association and made by A. G. Spalding & Bros.

The costumes of the players form another very important feature, and should be of a proper and serviceable nature. The pants should be made of canvas, drill or moleskin, and should be well padded at hips and knees. A strong guard should be worn to protect the thighs. A jersey should be used, well padded at the shoulders and elbows. The pads can be sewed on outside, or attached to the body, and when a jersey is put on, will help to hold them in place.

The stockings should be long, and of strong worsted, wool or cotton.

The most important feature of the entire uniform is the shoe. Ordinary street shoes, with leather cross-bars nailed on will do, but the regular foot ball shoe equipped with leather cleats, so arranged to help the player to start, stop or dodge, without slipping, made with a hard box toe, should fit the foot firmly, yet comfortably. The Mike Murphy ankle brace made in the shoe is an almost sure preventative of sprained ankles.

Head guards are made to protect the player and must not be made of sole leather, papier mache or any other hard, unyielding material that might injure another player.

The team of eleven men is usually divided into seven forwards or line men, consisting of a center, two guards, two tackles and two ends, who stand in a line facing their seven opponents and keep them away from the runner when on offense, and to break through opponents and down the runner when on defense; a quarter-back, who stands behind this line and usually directs the play of the team; two half-backs and a full-back, who play a few yards behind the quarter-back and are used as runners when in possession of the ball and defenders of the goal when the other side is in possession.

Before commencing practice, a man should be chosen to act as referee, umpire and linesman, for in practice games it is hardly necessary to have more than one official. The two sides then toss up, and the one winning the toss has choice of goal or kick-off. If there be a wind, the winner will naturally and wisely take the goal from which that wind is blowing and allow his opponent to have the ball. If there be no advantage in the goals he may choose the kick-off, and his opponents in that case take whichever goal they like. The two teams then line up, the holders of the ball placing it upon the middle of the 40-yard line of the kicker's side, 60 yards from the opponents' goal, and the opponents being obliged to stand back at least ten yards, until the ball has been touched with the foot. Some man of the side having the kick-off must then kick the ball at least ten yards into the opponents' territory. Preferably, therefore, he will send it just short of the goal line or as far as he can, and still have his forwards reach the spot in season to prevent too great headway being acquired by the opponents' interference, but he will not kick it across the side line. The opponents then catch it and return it by a kick, or they run with it. If one of them runs with it he may be tackled by the opponents. He may not, however, be tackled below the knees. As soon as the ball is fairly held, that is, both player and ball brought to a standstill, or the runner with the ball touches the ground with any part of his person, except his hands or feet, while in the grasp of an opponent, the referee blows his whistle and the runner has the ball "down," and someone upon his side, usually the man called the snap-back or center, must place the ball on the ground at that spot for a "scrimmage," as it is termed. The ball is then put in play again, placing it flat on the ground with its long axis parallel to the side line (while the men of each team keep on their own side of the ball, under the penalty of a foul for off-side play, a line parallel to the goal line and passing through the end of the ball nearest the side's own goal line determining the position of the players of each side) by the snap-back's snapping the ball back, either with his foot, or more commonly with his hands, to a player of his own side just behind him, who is called the quarter-back. The ball is in play, and both sides may press forward as soon as the ball is put in motion by the snap-back. Naturally, however, as the quarter-back usually passes it still further behind him to a half-back, or back, to kick or run with, it is the opposing side which is most anxious to push forward, while the side having the ball endeavor by all lawful means to retard that advance until their runner or kicker has had time to execute his play. It is this antagonism of desire on the part of both sides that has given rise to the special legislation regarding the use of the hands, body and arms of the contestants —and beginners must carefully note the distinction. As soon as the snap-back has sent the ball behind him, he has really placed all the men in his own line off-side; that is, between the ball and the opponents' goal, and they, therefore, can theoretically occupy only the position in which they stand, while the opponents have the legal right to run past them as quickly as possible. For this reason, and bearing in mind that the men "on side" have the best claim to right of way, it has been enacted that the side having possession of the ball may not use their hands or arms, but only their bodies, when thus off-side, to obstruct or interrupt their adversaries, while the side running through in the endeavor to stop the runner, or secure possession of the ball, may use their hands and arms to make passage for themselves. Nor may the side in possession of the ball form any locked interference by taking hold of each other, nor may they in any way push or pull their own man who is running with the ball. The game thus progresses in a series of downs, followed by runs, passes or kicks, as the case may be, the only limitation being that of a rule designed to prevent one side continuously keeping possession of the ball without any material advance or retreat, which would be manifestly unfair to the opponents. This rule provides that in four "downs" or attempts to advance the ball, a side not having made ten yards toward the opponents' goal must surrender possession of the ball. As a matter of fact, it is seldom that a team actually surrenders the ball in this way, because, after three attempts, if the prospects of completing the ten-yards gain appear small, it is manifestly politic to kick the ball as far as possible down the field, and such a method is more likely to be adopted than to make a last attempt by a run and give the enemy possession almost on the spot. In such an exigency, if a kick be made, the rules provide that it must be such a kick as to give the opponents fair and equal chance to gain possession of the ball and must go beyond the line of scrimmage unless stopped by an opponent. A player may also, under certain restrictions, carefully stated in the rules, make what is known as a forward pass, that is, throw the ball forward to another player of his own side. In case of a forward pass, the player making the pass must be at least 5 yards back of the line of scrimmage when doing this. There is one other element entering into this progress of the game, and that is the fair catch. This may be made from a kick by the opponents, provided the catcher indicates his intention by raising his hand in the air, takes the ball on the fly and catches it, not taking more than two steps in any direction and no other of his own side touches it. This entitles him to a free kick; that is, his opponents may not come within ten yards of the spot where he made the catch, while he (and his side) may retire such distance toward his own goal as he sees fit, and then make a punt or a drop, or give the ball to some one of his own side to place the ball for a place kick. Here again, as at kick-off, when taking the free kick, he must make an actual kick of at least ten yards, unless the ball is stopped by the opponents. His own men must be behind the ball when he kicks it, or be adjudged off-side. If he prefers, he may have the ball down for a scrimmage instead, and both teams line up for a scrimmage with center passing the ball.

Whenever the ball goes across the side boundary line of the field, it is said to go "into touch," or out of bounds, and it must be at once brought back to the point where it crossed the line, and then put in play by some member of the side which carried it out, or first secured possession of it after it went out. If the ball be kicked out of bounds or passed out of bounds, it belongs to the opponents at the point that it crosses side lines. The method of putting it in play is to take it to the spot where it crossed the line and then carry it at right angles into the field fifteen yards, unless preference for a different distance is stated, which, however, cannot be more than fifteen yards nor less than five from side line, and make an ordinary scrimmage of it, the same as after a down. We will suppose that the ball by a succession of these plays, runs, kicks, forward pass, downs, fair catches, etc., has advanced toward one or the other of the goals, until it is within kicking distance of the goal posts. The question will now arise in the mind of the captain of the attacking side as to whether his best plan of operation will be to try a drop-kick at the goal or forward-pass it, or to continue the running attempts, in the hope of carrying the ball across the goal line, for this latter play will count his side a touchdown, and entitle them to a try-at-goal.

In deciding, therefore, whether to try a drop-kick, forward pass, or continue the running attempts, he should reflect upon the value of the scores. The touchdown resulting from an end run or forward pass will count 6 points, even if he afterwards fails to convert it into a goal, by sending the ball over the bar and between the posts, while, if he succeed in converting it, the touchdown and goal together count 7 points. A drop-kick, if successful, counts 3 points, but is, of course, even if attempted, by no means sure of resulting successfully. He must, therefore, carefully consider all the issues at this point, and it is the handling of those problems that shows his quality as a captain. If he elects to continue his running attempts, and eventually carries the ball across the line, he secures a touchdown at the spot where the ball is finally held, after being carried over, and any player of his side may then bring it out, and when he reaches a suitable distance, place the ball for one of his side to kick, the opponents, meantime, standing behind their goal line. In placing the ball it is held in the hands of the placer, close to, but not touching the ground, and then carefully aimed until the direction is proper; the kicker himself may aim it, touching it with his hands, provided the ball does not touch the ground. Then, at a signal from the kicker that it is right, it is placed upon the ground, still steadied by the hand or finger of the placer, and instantly kicked by the place kicker. The reason for this keeping it off the ground until the last instant is that the opponents may charge forward as soon as the ball touches the ground, and hence would surely stop the kick if much time intervened. If the ball goes over the cross-bar the goal counts and the opponents then have the option of kick-off or receiving kick-off. If they decide to kick-off they do so from their own 40-yard mark, but should they decree to receive the kick-off the team scoring places the ball on their own 40-yard line and the game is continued by kicking the ball.

There is one other issue to be considered at this point, and that is, if the ball be in possession of the defenders of the goal, or if it fall into their hands when thus close to their own goal. Of course, they will naturally endeavor, by running or kicking, to, if possible, free themselves from the unpleasant situation that menaces them. Sometimes, however, this becomes impossible, and there is a provision in the rules which gives them an opportunity of relief, at a sacrifice, it is true, but scoring less against them than if their opponents should regain possession of the ball and make a touchdown or a goal. A player may at any time kick, pass or carry the ball across his own goal line, and there touch it down for safety. This, while it scores two points for his opponents, gives his side the privilege of bringing the ball out to the twenty-yard line, and then putting it down for a scrimmage.

The succession of plays continues for four periods of 15 minutes each. Between the second and third periods there intervenes a 15-minute intermission, after which the side which did not have the kick-off at the commencement of the match has possession of the ball for the kick-off. But between the first and second and third and fourth periods there is only a one-minute intermission, and the players of neither side are allowed to leave the field; the ends being changed, and the ball placed in the same relative position, the down and point to be gained remaining the same. The result of the match is determined by the number of points scored during the four periods, a goal from a touchdown counting 7 points; one from the field, that is, without the aid of a touchdown, 3 points; a touchdown from which no goal is kicked scoring 6 points, and a safety counting 2 points for the opponents. In practice it is usual to have the periods of play somewhat shorter than for a regular game.

How to Play Foot Ball

BY WALTER CAMP.

I wish to preface the brief remarks which I take occasion to make in this chapter regarding special plays in foot ball with the statement that they are not intended to cover the first principles of the individual positions in the game. In another book I have dwelt upon these at length, and have there defined with as great accuracy as I could the principal duties assignable to the occupant of each position on the team. In addition to this, I have there given the main features of team play. It is worth while to mention this at the outset, because a team can make no greater mistake than by taking up what are known as "trick" plays, or, in fact, any of the ordinary team plays in the present modern game, before the individuals of that team have become thoroughly perfected in the practical rudiments of the game, and perform almost by instinct the ordinary duties of their positions. This education in fundamentals has grown even more important in the past few years, for a team may no longer rely upon compactness of formation and the power of weight and concentration, because it is impossible by means of such plays to gain ten yards even in four downs. Hence education in individual perfection becomes more of a necessity than ever. A team which undertakes to make strategic plays before mastering these primary points will always find itself working at a tremendous disadvantage, and the waste of power will be almost incalculable. Perhaps I could not put it more plainly than to say that the tendency is altogether too much toward what is known as "git thar" principles in all of our lines of sport to-day. A crew endeavors to row in a shell before learning the principles of the stroke; our boxers are apt to go in for the swinging, knock-out blow at the sacrifice of the more old-fashioned, but better form, sparring; but in none of these forms is it more evident than in the one under discussion, namely, foot ball. It is not at all uncommon to see a team playing intricate criss-crosses, double and forward passes and concealed ball plays, whose men are still tackling high, and whose half-backs kick a punt from low down on the toe. To every reader of this book then, I say, with the heartiest good will, master the rudiments first if you wish to make yourself valuable to any team; master them thoroughly if you wish to see your team win when it comes to important matches. These special plays which follow are plays which captains and coaches can work out to an almost infinite number of variations, but it will be the individual players on the team who will, in the end, determine whether the use of these plays will turn out successfully.

Under the present rules, whenever a free kick is attempted, it must be an actual kick of not less than ten yards into the opponents' territory. The introduction of this rule caused all the flying wedge opening plays of some years ago, as well as formed wedges from fair catches to disappear. The captain now has to perform the principal part of his strategic play, outside of the kick, from ordinary downs, instead of from what have been called "free kicks," but what have been really "free wedges." Furthermore, the more recent changes in the rules make one of the prime essentials of a good team proficiency in running, forward passing and kicking from regular formations.

I, therefore, begin with running in the line. By this I mean running, from his position in the line, by any one of the six men of the forward line. This may prove a fair chance to to take at times under the new rules. Some years ago there was a great deal of guard running, and in a good many books published recently on the game, the guard is spoken of as the only available man in the line for running with the ball. That is true to this extent: The guard occupies a position for short and, perhaps, unexpected runs, but with the modern game the guard is such a feature in the defensive work that it has become a good deal of a question whether he ought to be given much running to do on his own account, and especially as he must now, from his position in the line. Many coaches do not allow their guards to run with the ball at all. Then, again, he can no longer be taken back into what is known as the guard-back formation, which was formerly his strongest ground-gaining play. But if the reader will bear this in mind, and so not make use of his guard except to such an extent as shall still preserve the guard for his line play, one can say that he has in these guards two available men in the line. The most natural run for the guard or tackle is outside of tackle, on the opposite side of the rush line from which he stands. In the performance of this run by the tackle, the principal feature is to disguise the fact that the tackle is about to start, and his getting a quick and free start, not followed, or followed at a considerable distance only by his vis-a-vis. In order to do this he must form the habit of holding himself in the same position when he is not going to make this run that he occupies when he is going to undertake it, for any difference will indicate to his opponent what the play is to be. But, breaking away, he runs closely behind the quarter-back, taking the ball on the fly as he passes, and making a short and sharp dash, just about over the tackle's position, who, with the assistance of the backs, all of whom precede the runner and break through ahead of him. A tackle may also be run in a similar fashion around the end, but this latter play is of no great value except with particularly fast tackles, and, more than that, it uses up the tackle's wind a good deal more than when he goes just outside of tackle, because the intereference is likely to stand out pretty well toward the edge of the field, and the tackle will run his full distance and not be able to get through the end after all, thus having taken a considerable dash at high speed and with no good result, but merely the loss of a down. In defining the tackle's running, I have also defined the running of the guard where he goes around behind the quarter in a similar fashion. These plays are strong where the guard is a big man and a hard runner with good legs. A fat man is useless in such a case. Some teams formerly performed some very excellent work in dropping guards back as interferers, and also in giving the guards themselves the ball occasionally. This is, of course, impossible now under the rules, as no line man may be dropped back, except when he takes up a position at least five yards in the rear of his line of scrimmage and a back goes up to his place in the line. The ends may be used exactly as the guards or tackles in running.

Other runs which are possible by the line men are, of course, criss-cross and delayed passes. One example of these criss-crosses will illustrate sufficiently to enable a captain or coach to carry out a great variety of them, using every man in his line if he wishes.

For instance, the tackle and half-back criss-cross. As in the instance I described of the ordinary tackle run, the tackle—say the left tackle—suddenly shakes himself free from his opponent and dashes straight at the quarter, a few feet behind him, of course; the quarter passes him the ball as he reaches him, exactly as though the left tackle were then going around between the right tackle and the guard. But instead of doing this, the left tackle passes to the right half, who runs to the left end, the half, full-back and quarter all interfering for him. The great point in this play is to see that the opposing right tackle does not get the runner as he starts off to get the ball, and furthermore, that this right tackle and right end are blocked late but long. Such a criss-cross can also be worked with the end, and with the guard it can also be tried to turn either inside or outside of the end. So much for the line men running. Wing shifts or line shifts, that is, plays wherein one side of the line shifts just before the ball is put in play over to the other side, are also becoming increasingly common.

Next we come to the half-backs and full-backs. Every one is familiar with the following plays, which we only mention in order to call them to the attention of the captain who is studying out in the early part of the season what plays he shall make the most of. The half-back running on his own side between any of the various men in the line; the half-back running between any of the men on the side away from his own side; the full-back running on the right side or the left side through the same openings and under the same circumstances and with practically the same interference, for in the modern game the captain is wise who uses his three men behind the line in such a way that any one of them may perform any of the various plays devised for the backs, and then maintain a similar formation, no matter what the play is to be. One cannot too strongly deprecate the exact detailing of certain movements in certain plays to get through or block or to take care of particular individuals when that move leads to the betrayal of the play before it has actually come off. The cardinal points to be remembered regarding running by the half-backs and full-backs are these: That the interference must depend upon the speed of the men engaged, and that no interference should be such as to slow up the runner appreciably, unless it be for some trick play or double pass where the slowing up of the runner means merely his being caught after getting rid of the ball. I have seen many a good team spoiled by their attempting to follow out a set rule as to the order in which interferers should reach the end. For instance, in the days of Heffelfinger, he showed how a guard could readily go from his own position out to the opposite end, and before the runner, and interfere most nobly for him all the way down the field. For this reason every guard was at once coached to go out and interfere on the end. Three out of five were too big and slow to accomplish this to any advantage, but that did not seem to make any difference. Somebody had written that the guard should interfere on the end, and the result was that everybody had to wait until the guard got out there. Meantime, the runner was usually caught from behind. A good guard who can pick up his feet lively, and who can get around quickly and easily after blocking, can get out before an ordinarily fast runner. A team ought not to have a quarter-back who is too slow to get out to the end as an interferer before the back with the ball reaches the other point. But for all that there are quarter-backs, and good ones, too, who are a little slow in this and hold back the runner. These men should either be coached into better speed or taught a little different way of getting rid of the ball—on the run, perhaps—or be sent to perform the tackle's duties, and let the tackle get there if the tackle is a remarkably fast man; otherwise such a transfer would only make bad worse. From what I have already said the captain can see that he must measure his interference by the speed of his interferers, and match them with the speed of his runner with the ball in order to satisfactorily solve the equation for his own team. It is the captain of brains who wins by doing just these things, while the captain without them takes the hard and fast rule that has been laid down by some one, perhaps of his own team, who has written an article from the knowledge of only one or two teams, and thinks that all can be brought up to exactly the same point in the same way.

Regarding going through the line close to the center by backs (and by backs I mean the quarter and half-backs as well), there are two ways of sending a man through the line. One is to batter a hole before him and let him slip through, and the other is to put him through a quick opening. There are line plays which combine a variety of these tactics, but there are some principles to be remembered in connection with them which will give them something more than a careless "hit or miss" move. In the first place, a big, heavy man should never be run into the line with one or two light interferers preceding him, whereas a light man can be run in behind two heavy men with abandon. The reason for this is that there are times when the hole will be choked up in spite of the attempt of the interferers, and a heavy man getting his head down may strike one of the interferers in the back and incapacitate him for future work. It is not so apt to hurt the runner as it is the man whom he strikes, although there have been cases of injury to the runner. When the hole is choked up, and heavy men are interfering, they can usually keep the mass moving away from the runner, even if they do not open the hole for him, and this play is much less hard and far less dangerous. In sending two light interferers ahead to spring an opening for the runner, it should be borne in mind that an opening made in this way is a quick, sharp one, and should be utilized instantly. An opening, on the other hand, made by two heavy men in this fashion can be much smaller and rely largely upon the accumulated force even after the runner strikes the line. The men who go ahead to interfere must always remember if they have to go down to fall away from the opening and not block it up.

To come now to the wedges or mass plays. Owing to the

prejudice of the public and the feeling that wedge work was taking too much of the attention of the players, captains and coaches, the rule-makers attempted to eliminate a great deal of this work by the passage of a rule against momentum-mass plays as well as the passage of a rule insisting upon actual kicks. This latter rule I have mentioned earlier in this book. There is no question but that this has done away with a great deal of the most showy part of the flying wedge, but rules against momentum-mass playing had not and are not likely to eliminate the use of the principle of wedges. They took off the weight which it was possible to get into these wedges, and in that way were an excellent thing, but it required more severe legislation to eliminate all mass plays. This, however, was accomplished quite effectively by the ten-yard rule adopted. The addition of the rule forbidding pushing and pulling and locked interference completed the demolition of the old mass play.

The development of the position of quarter-back, so far as running is concerned, has been toward the old rules, when many years ago it was possible for the man receiving the ball from the snap-back to carry it forward. Some years since a rule was enacted again permitting the quarter-back to run, provided, however, he went out at least five yards from the point at which the ball was snapped. The first season this permission did not offer any very great developments along the line, but, like any other play of this nature, seems to be developing in the hands of the coaches and players until it promises to be a considerable feature of the game. The continuation of the quarter-back run with the forward pass also offers excellent opportunities for successful play. It is interesting because it admits of greater possibilities, and a run of this nature, when it is thoroughly successful, develops into spectacular play which pleases the spectator and demands one more qualification in a quarter-back.

Now, with the privilege allowed the quarter-back of crossing the line of scrimmage at any point, there are many more of these runs attempted.

There are several methods of effecting the quarter-back run, and although naturally it is difficult to bring it off unless it is performed unexpectedly, it does lend itself to the development of interference. The usual method is for the interference to circle outside of tackle, the quarter-back protected by the interferers making a very direct run out toward the end and circling as his interferers turn in.

Another method is to pass the ball back apparently to the full-back for a kick, and he acting, as will be seen, as a quarter-back, may run with the ball out around the end. Forward passing by any man back of the line is allowable.. The man making the pass must be five yards back of the line of scrimmage.

To come to the last point of this brief summary of plays, namely, kicking. This department under the present rules becomes still more important, even though a field-kick goal counts now but three points. The special points about kicking are the accurate placing of the ball and the acquirement of short and long-distance punting as well as place kicking. Kicking into touch, where admissible under the rules, should be made much more of, and it is becoming absolutely necessary for a team to have good punters. To go into the details of these kicks would be an almost infinite task, but the captain can study out the situation from the following premises: A kick is absolutely necessary at kick-off, and often after fair catch. What kind of a kick, then, will be most advantageous to his team? A short one, high, where his man can get under it, or a long-distance one, giving the opponents a chance, perhaps, of return, but enabling him, if he has fast ends, to hold the ball down at the distance of the kick? How best shall he take advantage of all his possibilities?

Kicking has thus come to be an absolute essential in a well-rounded team, and the style of that kicking adapted to the make-up of the individual components of that team in end rushers, tackles and backs.

Modern Attack and Forward Pass

The coach must make up his mind that while it is absolutely useless to rely upon hammering plays to win games, he must develop some fairly consistent short ground-gaining plays and a full repertoire of open plays, forward passes and on-side kicks.

The open play, that is, taking big chances of wide end runs or surprises combined with the forward pass, must still make up the threatening attacking force of an eleven to-day. But this does not mean that line bucking should be forgotten. There is apt to come a time in any game when the team must carry that ball for fifteen yards with certainty, when line bucking is a very valuable asset, and they must be tried out in doing this and tested until the coach feels that they will not be found wanting in a pinch. Now, it is not the simplest thing in the world to accomplish this, but it is not impossible by any means.

Elsewhere in this book the detail of the running play is sufficiently dwelt upon so that it is more important to discuss the points of the forward pass.

First, it is well to consider this as the means of alarming the opponents and forcing them to place their defense in such a position as to make it more possible to puncture their line or circle their ends. When the forward pass first came in very few teams realized that there was any other way to frighten the opponents than by actually making the pass. Teams now have learned, however, that it is quite possible to alarm the opponents and open out their defense without taking a chance of surrendering the ball, which is likely to happen on any forward pass that is not recovered by the attacking side. With this end in view, it is wise to have a certain line of plays primarily based upon the half-back or back charging around the end of the line, in which play the end himself goes forward, turning toward his runner and extending his arms as if to take the pass. Meantime the back, who is running, still circling back after having received the ball, puts it in such a position in his hand as if he were getting ready to make a forward pass, but still runs on (see illustration 4 in Plate VII.) Now, it is impossible under these conditions for the opponents to know whether the man actually intended to make the pass and then found that the position of his end or his own progress was such as to make it inadvisable to complete the pass, or whether it was a fake play all the way through. As, therefore, it was impossible for the opponents to tell they must guard just as though the pass had been made, and hence their line of defense has been weakened by it, and again they may be rendered nervous for fear the next time the man will pass the ball.

Now as to the detail of forward passes and kicks themselves when actually made. A forward pass may be made in a variety of ways. When the play was first started the men passed the ball in any old fashion. A toss end over end, a swing like that used by the quarter-back in making a long side pass, or even a two-handed pitch like a toss of a basket ball. As men became more familiar with the use of their hands in manipulating these passes, they found that a good deal more could be done than was at first contemplated. This was on account of the shape of the ball. It was found that a man could throw the ball as one would a spear or javelin, and this, in addition to the side swing or spiral, made it possible to do a great deal in the way of distance and accuracy. The spiral pass is the only one used today. The ball may be held underneath with its point forward and the fingers over the lacing and driven forward with almost the same motion that a ball is pitched for an outcurve in base ball (see illustration No. 3 in Plate VI). The overhand pass may be used for longer distance. The ball is held back of the middle, between the thumb and fingers, with the fingers on the lacing. The ball is grasped firmly and the position is like that of an overhand throw in base ball. The ball is driven forward, the grasp of the fingers on the lacing and the thumb on the ball causing the ball to fly with a spiral or turning motion with its long axis continually pointed forward and horizontal to the ground (see illustration No. 3 in Plate IV).

In order for a team to meet with success in completing forward passes, it is absolutely necessary that some deception is used to throw the opposing team off its guard, such as employing a double or delayed pass in the back-field before the forward pass is attempted; the throwing of the ball in the opposite direction in which the play has started, or the making of the pass from a running formation, for it is next to impossible to complete a forward pass if your opponents have any surety of the pass being made.

As a scoring play, the forward pass completed behind the goal line has been used with much success.

How to Play the Line Positions

BY TOM THORP.

The most important department of foot ball, and perhaps the one that in many instances is given the least amount of attention, is the one that calls for the systematic play of the men who constitute what is termed the "rush line" of the team.

This peculiar state of affairs is traceable in two ways: First, to the fact that the majority of coaches selected at the various colleges are, for the most part, men who occupied positions in rear of the line of scrimmage during their collegiate days, and consequently are not as well versed in the requirements of line play as in the other departments of the game; and, second, that line play, to many coaches, appears worthy of nothing more than a hasty outline of the duties of the position to qualify candidates to play them properly.

Either of the above reasons are sufficient to prove the inability of a coach to turn out a well-balanced, smooth-running machine. Many of the colleges are, therefore, safeguarding their foot ball candidates from any such state of affairs, by engaging both line and back-field coaches.

True it may be that only one particle of the diamond does the cutting, but those behind it help and the most distant one in the gem co-operates with it. Without them, the point would be inert and the cutting impossible. So it is with the game of foot ball. A team is composed of eleven players, all working in conjunction with one another, and if one fails to do his respective share, the strength of the combination is broken up, with the result that victory is generally denied them.

Very often a team composed of a fast, hard-playing back-field and a slow, unsupporting line, will display remarkable scoring strength when confronted by light and weaker rivals, but when put to the acid test, its strength against an eleven of superior line men and a back-field of only ordinary ability, it will be found that its scoring power will be greatly diminished

1, Proper way to block in the open. Throwing a shoulder into opponent thus carrying him off his feet. 2, Blocking from the rear. Throw body across legs of opponent. 3, "Boxing tackle" by end. This block must be made fast and hard or else effectiveness will be greatly diminished. Other line men may employ above method in opening holes. 4, Illustrates the pinning to the ground of player by interferer.

PLATE I

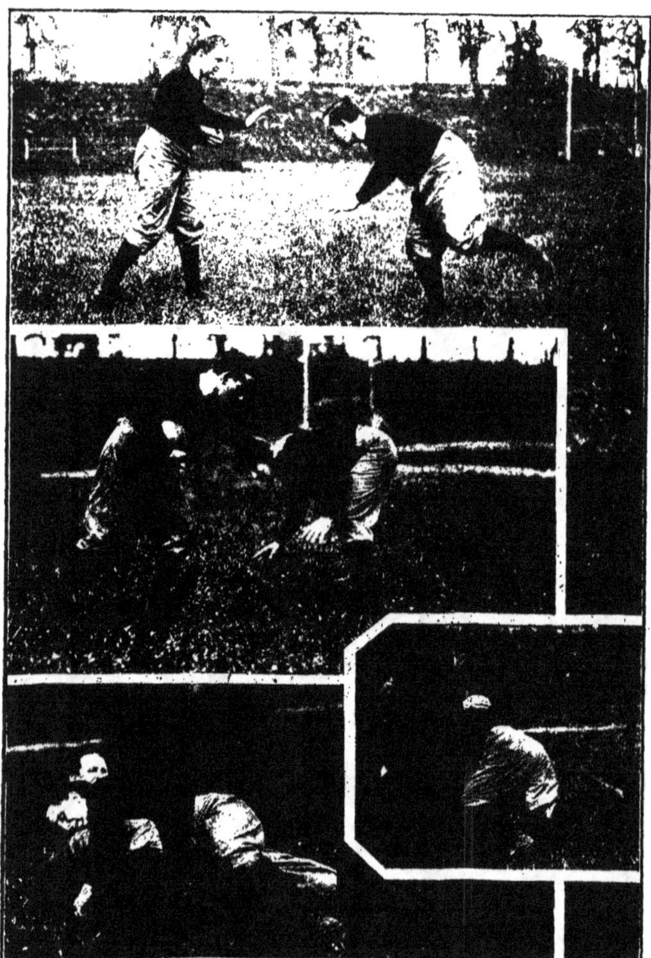

1 and 2, "Straight-arming" of tackler in open. As tackler approaches the ball is changed so that the free arm will be on the side toward tackler. Arm extended, and as tackler closes in he is warded off by the free use of hand. 3, Tackling is one of the fine arts of foot ball. Every tackle should be sure and certain. Opponents should be hit slightly above the knees with the shoulder, arms encircling legs. 4, If the tackle is properly made the opponent will be thrown on his back or to the side. If improperly made, the tackler will be carried along by opponent.

PLATE II

by the mediocre play of the line men, and instead of being considered a strong combination, will be classed as a weak and ill-assorted squad of performers.

Line play is just as important a factor in team strength as back-field ability, and the sooner a coach realizes this, the easier will be his task of developing the proper combination of team play necessary to success.

In order to develop a squad along the proper lines, it is absolutely necessary to teach all of the respective candidates the self-same rudiments of the game. No matter whether it is a center, guard, tackle, end, half or full-back, each and every candidate must be given a thorough knowledge of the fundamental principles of the game. Ability to bring into play, at any time in a contest, the proper knowledge of these principles contributes much to the success of a team.

Falling on the ball, catching kick-offs, punts, drop-kicks or place kicks; tackling opponents in the open, as well as the ability to down them in an attempt to penetrate the line or circle the end; blocking or picking off opponents in the open or on the line of scrimmage; throwing or receiving forward passes or intercepting them, or interfering for the man with the ball, are all requirements that must be mastered to a degree of perfection by all candidates alike, before they can be considered far enough advanced to be taught the functions of team play. In fact, many more exactions fall upon the men who make up the forward line of a team than on their brother players behind the line, but all of the above essentials must be instilled in them before any of the details of their position can be taken up.

In endeavoring to lay out some proper road to success in foot ball, the following line of procedure may be advanced as the only one that will ultimately bear the just fruits of a coach's efforts:

First: Assemble the candidates, dividing them into squads of ten or twelve, placing the veterans in the front ranks of each squad and thus afford the novices a chance of seeing how each veteran performs all the rudiments; drill each and every man in the proper way to fall on the ball; perfect them in this until every man can recover a ball whether it is thrown at him, from him, to his right or left, or whether on the run or from a standing position (see illustration 2 in Plate III). Too much time cannot be spent in teaching this important fundamental, as hundreds of games have been won or lost by the ability or inability of an individual player to properly recover a fumbled ball or blocked kick. Candidates may also be drilled in the recovering of bounding balls, by teaching them to pick up a ball on the run, as in base ball, instead of falling on it. At some colleges, falling on the ball is only resorted to when it is absolutely necessary and not when a ball has bounded free in the open. Sammy White's famous runs in the Harvard and Yale games resulted from his ability to recover a free ball in the open without leaving his feet.

Second: The proper way to catch, throw or pass a ball should be taught.

Many different methods are in vogue for teaching candidates the above requirements. To catch a ball with the least possible chance for a fumble is best done by what is known as the "basket form" catch. This consists in, first, properly judging the ball while in the air. (Might add here that too much practice in judging kicks or passes cannot be indulged in). After the judging has been properly taken care of, the catcher places himself in such a position so that he will be under the ball and not wait so that he will be forced to make the catch while on the run (see illustration 3 in Plate III).

Many costly fumbles have resulted from the failure of a player to get under the ball immediately and allow himself plenty of time to make the catch. After getting to the proper spot to make the catch, on the right or left side, raising the arms toward the ball in a basket-like form, using the outside arm as the uppermost part of the basket and the other as the bottom or other side, he should allow the ball to strike his body, but not on the chest, which always results in a fumble, but on the part just below the chest, at the same time be tightening the arms around the ball. A good plan is to exercise the body and legs, so that they may become part of the catch, by allowing them to give way the least appreciable bit with the ball (see illustration 4 in Plate III).

On kick-offs the ball may be caught on the run, thus enabling the catcher to get into his stride faster and gain considerably more ground. Catching a ball on the run in this manner also affords the catcher more opportunity to dodge an oncoming tackler, but should only be employed by the experienced player, who is sure of holding the ball.

In carrying the ball on the run the player should be absolutely certain of a tight hold upon it, so that when he is tackled the ball will not be fumbled. To do this, one point of the ball should be held firmly in the palm of the hand with the other point snugly fitted into the armpit (see illustration 1 in Plate IV). The other hand may be employed to ward off tacklers or to break the fall to the ground when thrown (see illustration 3 in Plate II).

Throwing the ball or passing the ball has, in this era of forward passing, become a very important function. The ball should be placed in the palm of the hand, with the fingers grasping the lace side, rear part, and the thumb on the inside. The hand should then be carried back, so that the ball is at the height of the head. The fingers and thumb are used as the driving and controlling powers, respectively. The ball should be thrown in the same manner as a base ball, by shooting the arm forward in a snappy motion. The pass should be sharp, fast and straight, and not a long oval one. Of course, where great distance is to be required, the necessary height must be allowed, but never must the ball be allowed to soar in the air, as this results in a slow oval pass, giving the opponents sufficient time to either intercept the pass or else spoiling the pass by batting it to the ground (see illustration 3 in Plate IV).

Third: Tackling, blocking, picking off opponents or interfering for the man with the ball, all come under the same requirements.

Tackling is a department in foot ball that ranks second to none and should demand from both coach and players a special amount of attention. A team composed of a squad of sure tacklers is the hardest aggregation to defeat. Deadly tackling will take more ginger and fight out of an opponent than any other thing known on the gridiron, especially if the tackle is made after a long run. Also, less danger is encountered by a player if he tackles an opponent viciously than if he only made a half-hearted attempt and failed to bring him down with a thud (see illustration 4 in Plate II).

A tackling dummy should be employed in the preliminary work. Ability to leave one's feet and strike an opponent with the shoulder is more easily acquired with the aid of a dummy than by any other method.

The dummy should be hung in a place so situated that the players are afforded a clear run at it from all angles. The candidates should then be instructed to approach the dummy at a moderate rate of speed and when within four or five feet of it to hurl their bodies at it, carrying the head and shoulders to the front, striking the form at about the height of the thighs with the point of the shoulder, encircling the legs with the arms, so that when it is knocked from its fastenings, it will be carried forward, firmly pinned in the arms of the tackler (see illustrations 3 and 4 in Plate II).

The men should be coached to launch their bodies at the supposed opponent, first from the right and then from the left foot, with the speed moderate at first, but increasing gradually so that it will be possible for them to make the tackle from either foot without any hesitancy, when going at any rate of speed.

Another method that should be taught, especially to line candidates, is that of not only completing a hard tackle from a run, but to do likewise when at a standstill, as will often be necessary when a back attempts to plunge through the line.

This method differs somewhat from the one already described, inasmuch as the shoulder is thrown into an opponent a little above the knee, and, instead of encircling the legs with the arms, the hands are carried down almost to the back of the shoe tops; then, by using the shoulder as a fulcrum and applying the power with the hands, the opponent is thrown heavily backward. In this kind of a game, where the man carrying the ball is not allowed the assistance of his teammates to push or pull him on, as in the old game, this style of tackling for a line man will prove very effective. Another method is to have the tackle throw his body across the path of an oncoming runner and grasp him about the knees with the arms.

Blocking opponents is more an acquired knack of getting in the way of an opponent than anything else. The candidates must remember that the most effective thing to employ in blocking is the human body. An arm or hand is very easily brushed aside and will generally draw a penalty from an official, while the weight of the body is a load in itself sufficient to check the progress of an opponent when hurled at him; striking him at the knees or thereabouts, it is sure to bring him to earth (see illustration 1 in Plate I).

Picking off opponents, as well as interfering for a runner, are a great deal the same to the one used in blocking, only in the latter case the body is always launched in such a manner as to cross the path of the opponent. In case the judgment of the distance is short, the opponent will have to jump over or go around the prostrated form to get to the ball, thus giving the man with the ball an opportunity of going out or cutting inside to avoid the tackler; picking off a man from the rear, as in illustrations 2 and 4 in Plate I, is also a good method to employ.

All of the above fundamentals must be perfected in the individuals before they are to be taught any of the details of their positions.

As quarter-back and the other back-field positions are taken care of in much detail in other parts of this book, I will not touch upon their duties in any way, but will confine myself in detailing the necessary qualifications of the positions that make up the "rush line" of the team.

CENTER.

A number of persons fail to appreciate the real value of a strong, fast pivot man. I use the term pivot because of the fact that I consider the man who occupies this important position, if he plays the game as it should be played, as nothing more or less than the pivot upon which the team revolves. If he proves to be slow and slovenly his teammates will lack fight and aggressiveness, where if he is full of life and snap, his mates will show the influence of these good qualities by being a fast, hard, playing aggregation. Therefore, it devolves upon the coach to make a suitable selection for this keystone position.

A man not too tall or ungainly, but one who is built close to the ground, yet not handicapped with unnecessary weight, should be selected. The day of the stout, beefy center has passed into the discards. It may be well to add that two center men should be kept in constant training, since very often a serious injury to the regular will necessitate the playing of the substitute, and if none are available, the strength of the team will be crippled more by this scarcity than by the enforced absence of any other player.

The candidate should be instructed in the proper way to pass the ball to the quarter, half-backs and the kicker, by having him place the ball out in front of himself, bend over, so that a clear view of things in rear of the line of scrimmage is obtained by him; then with the steadiness of the "Rock of Gibraltar" type, pass the ball back to the quarter, backs in formation, and the kicker (see illustration 3 in Plate V).

After the center has acquired the knack of taking a steady position by constant practice, he should be drilled in making the pass to the quarter (see illustration 1 in Plate VIII). This may be done by a short snap-back motion, or by placing the ball in the quarter's hands. Both methods are employed, and it rests with the coach as to which one he prefers. After this, the long, direct pass to the kicker, as well as the shorter one to the backs in formation positions should be tried. All of these passes should be practised so that it will be next to impossible for a bad pass to result.

On offense, although the center has his head buried to a certain degree, he has the advantage over his opponent, in that he knows exactly when the ball is going to be snapped and at what point the play is directed. He should, therefore, manage to get the jump on the opposing center man and put him out of the play (see illustration 2 in Plate V). A center who allows an opponent to charge through him and spill a play in rear of the line of scrimmage should be sent to the side lines (see illustration 4 in Plate V).

Where the man with the ball does not have the assistance of his teammates to push and pull him on for the extra yards, the forwards are called upon to play a far different game than of old. They must take care of the secondary defense of the opponents, along with their opposing line men. The center must therefore, after putting his man out of the play, continue through with his second effort and pick off one of the trio of players that go to make up the secondary defense of the opposing team. The man backing up the center of the line of scrimmage is generally the one singled out for the center to pick off.

On defense, the centers of to-day play what is termed a "roving game." He stands about one and a half or two yards back of his place in the line, making every play inside of end safe and at the same time acting as a secondary defensive man when end runs are resorted to, but goes up into his rush line when opponents take a kick formation. It is quite similar to the old quarter-back position in the old style game, only when a kick formation is taken, he closes up the hole in the line and attempts to go through and block the kick. Body defense should be the style of his game, except when he has a clear try at the man with the ball. In line play he will find that a clear try is seldom allowed him, while in getting to the ball when end runs are used, he will generally have a free try at the man carrying the ball, provided, of course, that some line man has picked off the interference before the man reaches the line of scrimmage.

GUARDS.

There are two types of guards in foot ball. One is called the "Stand up Waiting Guard," the other the "Charging Guard." The offense of both are quite the same. They only vary in their defensive work. The "Stand up Waiting Guard," on defense, checks his man with his hands or shoulder, then diagnoses the play and finally gets to it. The "Charging Guard," on defense, by the use of hands or body, goes through into his opponents territory two or three yeards, finds the play and then closes in on it. The tall, rangy man is best adapted to the first style game, while the short, stocky player finds the latter style of play best suited to his build.

On offense, all line men play close to one another, leaving no holes in their line, but at the same time they make their individual bodies take up as much room as possible, without assuming a position in which they may very easily be bowled over (see illustrations 2, 3, 4 and 5 in Plate VIII). A good position to take is much similar to one a duck takes when it walks. It may be described as follows: Assuming a sprinter's start, with the knees opened a little wider than this position calls for so that the body may be close to the ground; butts low, head up and not buried; shoulders squared, with the back straight and forming an angle of about sixty degrees to the ground; eyes open, watching the opponent and the ball, ready to get the jump with the snap of the ball and throw a shoulder up into an opponent, carrying him back out of the range of the play. Line men do not start from the knee, but should always be on their toes and start with the snapping of the ball.

What was said of the center on offense as to his duty in caring for one of the defensive backs, also holds good for the guards, except when the guards are used to lead the interference, as in an end run. Then, of course, he cuts back between his own line and quarter-back, swings out wide, taking the first man he encounters. In quick openings and cross-bucks, his duty is to pick off one of the defensive backs. In making openings for his backs to gain through, guards, as well as all line men, must remember that they are to get their bodies between the man they are blocking and the man carrying the ball.

On defense, the use of the hands are allowed all players, therefore they should avail themselves of this advantage by using a hand to check or push an opponent aside to get to the ball. Nothing moves so fast as a hand. Guards are required to make all plays directed at their line safe, as well as to back up the extremities of the line.

TACKLES.

Tackles should be the most versatile men on the rush line. They should be selected because of their weight, speed and stamina, as well as their ability to be cool and collected at all times.

The duties that devolve upon the man playing this position are such, that to play it properly, one should have had the experience of at least one season. A tackle should be so familiar with line play that in case of emergency he would be able to jump in and play any of the other positions, except, perhaps, that of center.

Tackles, like all other line men, play in close to their inside man and not allow any holes in their scrimmage line (see illustration 5 in Plate VIII), and at the same time broaden out the line so that the backs will be afforded ample protection from the opponents. They must also be able to assist their ends in disposing of the opposing tackles on end runs, cross-bucks and straight openings through tackle.

The position that a tackle assumes depends to a great extent upon the style of play resorted to by the man opposite him. If the defensive guard plays close to his own center, then the tackle may be more free to go out for an opposing tackle; but if the guard persists in playing wide, the duty of the tackle is most difficult. He must make everything inside of him safe, and at the same time be in a position to lend a helping hand to his end in disposing of the opposing tackle on end runs, cross-bucks, and quick opening directed at his side of the line.

The same duty in reference to taking care of the secondary defense on all plays directed at the opposite side of his line holds for the tackle as for the center and guard. Only his efforts are directed at one or the other of the defensive flank men.

On defense he plays about two yards outside of his own guard, faces in toward the opposing backs, charges through into the opponents' territory with the snap of the ball, finds the play and gets his body across it, or else when afforded a clear try at the man with the ball, makes the tackle (see illustration 4 in Plate VIII). Very often inexperienced men will try to make the tackle rather than to cut off the interference. This is a very grave mistake. All interference should be picked off before the play gets to the end or back, otherwise a substantial gain will surely result. A tackle never backs up his own line, but follows all play in rear of his opponents' line, making all double and delayed passes impossible.

On kicks and forward passes he charges through, thereby hastening the kick or pass by his closeness to block the ball (see illustration 3 in Plate VII).

Tackles should acquire the knack of using their hands on defense. They should also vary their tactics of charging through their opponents so that their style will be such that the man trying to stop them will not know what to expect each time. A shoulder now, a straight arm then, and a charge around with a complete mowing down of an opponent will assist a tackle in getting through into the opposing territory.

ENDS.

This position calls more for the seasoned, quick thinking, catlike player than any of the others. An end must be a player who has a whirl of speed when going down the field under kicks, a beehive spring when opponents attempt to get by him, and a faculty of diagnosing a play almost before it has been started.

He should be a sure, hard tackler, never missing an opportunity to bring an opponent to earth, either in the open or on a play massed at his extremity of the line.

On offense, an end is called upon to make the space, separating himself from his tackle, safe as well as being able to box in or out the opposing tackle.

His exact position on offense and defense depends to a great extent on the style of play used by the opponents, though on offense he should place himself so that his outside foot will always occupy a space on the outside of the defensive tackle, except when the tackle is so foolish as to go out so far that he will be unable to safely play the space separating himself from his own guard. In such a case the end will stay within a foot or so of his own tackle and direct his quarter to concentrate his attack on this opening, thus bringing the tackle in, or else allowing his backs to gain considerable distance through the opening.

On defense, an end spreads out, playing from three to six yards from his own tackle, according to the end and type of defense adopted. "Waiting End," wide and a "Smashing End" close, he always turns a play in and never lets a runner get outside of him.

Two styles of play are possible for end men, namely, the "Smashing, Dashing End," who charges through in the direction of the opposing backs, hemming them in with the tackles in a half circle effect, or else the "Waiting End," who jumps five or six feet into opponents' territory at right angles to the line of scrimmage and then goes in to meet the play, turning everything in for the rest of the rush line and secondary defense to take care of, or else, if the interference is taken out by his tackle, downs the man with the ball. An end never goes behind his own line, but follows opponents' play behind their own line. If, however, the man with the ball has crossed the line of scrimmage on the opposite side of the line, he may cut across in back of his own line and make the tackle. This is because it is considered bad foot ball for the man with the ball, after once getting across the line of scrimmage, to turn back and run towards his own goal. Both styles of ends are being used at a great many colleges.

Covering kicks is a function of end play that all candidates must excel in. To master this properly, it takes hours of constant coaching as well as days of consistent practice. The end must be a sure tackler, have abundance of speed, and be a good judge of the carrying distance of kicks.

The positions of ends going down under kicks are: First, leave their positions and go out from five to ten yards closer to the side line. This will make the opposing men, whose duty it is to block them from going down the field, work more on their own responsibility and afford the end a much better chance of getting a fast, uninterfered-with start, and will assist the end in driving the man with the ball down the center of the field, so that the remainder of the team will be afforded an opportunity to down him, if he himself is kept from making the tackle.

As soon as the ball is snapped an end should be off with it, getting up his maximum speed as soon as possible, at the same time sidestepping or avoiding an opponent by the use of his hands. He should run without any reference to the ball until he has heard the thud of the kicker's foot against the ball. He should then glance over his inside shoulder, judge the ball, get control of his body, and at the same time close in sharply on the man who is to make the catch. If he is fortunate enough to get to the spot before the ball has been caught, he should not in any way interfere with the catch, but take up a position directly in front of, and a trifle to the outside of catcher, so that as soon as the ball has struck the opponent he may be able to leave his feet and tackle. If the ball is fumbled, he should either fall upon it or else recover it, and continue down the field with the ball until tackled.

Summing up the duties of the line on offense and defense they are as follows:

On offense the line plays close together; guards may lock legs with the center if they so wish; tackles close to guards and ends likewise; line not to be bundled up in a narrow mass, but each line man spreading himself out individually, so that he takes up as much room as possible without allowing his opponents to push him back or thrust him aside; line charges with ball as a stone wall, with no openings for opponents to sift through; each player with his head up and not buried; eyes open; butts low and shooting a shoulder up into an opponent, carrying him back out of the range of the play.

On defense the line spreads out; guards a yard or so from their center; tackles two or more yards; ends three to six yards, according to the end and type of defense adopted; body defense when play directed at line, except when clear chance at the man with the ball, then a sure, hard tackle; ends turning everything in, not allowing anyone to circle them.

Then remember the three final duties of all line men on defense: First, charge through into opponents' territory; second, find the play; third, get the body across it or make the tackle.

On kick formation it is the duty of line men to block opponents from sifting through the line, or else the kick will be blocked or shortened by considerable distance, by being hastened by the line man coming through.

If all of the above requirements are drilled into the candidates, they will no doubt be able to give very good accounts of themselves. As a last parting shot, it is for the line men to remember that too much effort cannot be expended in perfecting oneself in the rudiments of the game.

Play of the Backs

By W. T. Reid, Jr.,
Former Harvard Full-back and Head Coach.

Properly speaking, the term "backs" refers to the quarter-back, the two half-backs and the full-back. This article, however, will deal only with the three latter positions, leaving the very technical work of the quarter-back to some other writer.

The three backs, as we shall term them, are closely associated in everything that they do. On the offense they alternate in carrying the ball and interfering for one another, making forward passes or receiving them, also two of them should be able to execute an on-side kick. On the defense at least two of them, and sometimes all three, are called upon to reinforce the rush line and at the same time protect against forward passes and on-side kicks. And they are usually of about the same size and weight.

With all these points of similarity there is much that belongs to each separate position that goes to make it unwise for a back to attempt to play in more than one position. For instance, if the right half attempts to play at left half he must accustom himself to the use of the right side of his body in interference instead of his left, to starting toward the right side of the line for many of his main plays instead of to the left, to receiving the ball from the quarter-back from another angle, and in general to an almost exactly opposite way of doing things from that to which he has been accustomed. From these observations it must be clear that while the duties of the various positions are just different enough to make it unwise to change players about, they are nevertheless so nearly alike fundamentally as to make it possible to deal with them as a whole, thereby saving much repetition and unnecessary explanation.

QUALIFICATIONS.

The mental qualifications of a good back are first of all that he shall enter into his work with the proper spirit. Unless he has this spirit—that is, unless he is willing to subordinate his personal wishes to the general welfare of the team, and what is more, to do so heartily and enthusiastically—he cannot hope ever to be a great player, even though he has marked individual ability along every line of play. Team play is the essence of successful foot ball, and he who is looking first of all to his own interests will never make a "team" player; he will not contribute his share to the *esprit de corps* of the backs, and he will never "fight" for all he is worth from the beginning of a game until the end.

Besides having the proper spirit he should be heartily co-operative; he should be full of aggressiveness both on the offense and defense; full of sand and grit, and imbued with a reasonable amount of judgment. Physically, a back should be compactly built, strong and quick, never slow nor clumsy, and should weigh anywhere from 170 to 190 pounds. Possibly now it is not necessary to have such heavy backs, owing to the fact that with the advent of the 10-yard rule the plunging game is not so essential. However, when the ball must be carried over the latter portion of the field by a limited number of men—the necessity for one heavy, powerful back to do this, must be evident. In earlier days, before the defensive side of the game came to be so well understood, and before special styles of defense were devised to meet special forms of offense—it was generally planned to have at least one of the backs a good end runner. This provision is, under the new rules, likely to become quite as important now as it once was, owing to the fact that push-plays are no longer allowed. The defense has, however, mastered the end running game, unless indeed it consists of skillfully devised conception. The new rules have brought end running in again to a considerable extent. Hence, it is well for teams of to-day to choose for backs, those men who can as nearly as possible perform the task of the line man of the past two or three years. If, in meeting these requirements, an end runner turns up—well and good. Finally, the back should have the knack of not getting hurt. Some men have this to a marked degree, and almost never get hurt, while others are equally unfortunate and are constantly being injured. As team play is dependent upon "drill," and that in its turn is dependent upon the individual, it is easy to see why an "immune" back is most desirable.

FUNDAMENTAL POINTS.

Too much emphasis cannot be placed upon the necessity for thorough drill in fundamentals. These fundamentals consist of falling on the ball, passing it, kicking, catching and carrying it.

"Falling on the ball," or, more properly speaking, falling around the ball, should be practised while the ball is at rest, and then, while it is in motion, to the right, left, front and rear. In any case the player should be very careful not to dive at it in such a way as to dive the top of his shoulder into the ground, for a bad bruise or injury is likely to result.

Neither should he ever attempt to fall flat upon the ball lest he bring about an injury to his wind or his chest; instead, he should fall flat, either so that his weight shall be on his elbows or knees, or else so that his body at his waist is doubled up around the ball, which he shall hug closely with his arms and hands.

In diving for the ball the player should dive as closely to the ground as possible, thus preventing an opponent from getting under him. He should always see to it that his body is between the ball and an opponent. These points make for added safety and protection.

Backs should have enough practice in passing and throwing the ball to one another to feel thoroughly at home with them. This is especially true under the new rules. They cannot be sure of this unless they handle new balls, wet balls, old balls and dry balls, and unless they handle them incessantly.

Unless this is the case a team is likely to find itself without a kicker, perhaps in the midst of some important game. And the ordinary need for a kicker has been increased greatly by the changes in the rules, which make it necessary to advance the ball in gains of 10 yards even in four downs, with only four men behind the line—which is, of course, a much slower and less powerful way than that practised before. Here it is that a superior kicker can be of inestimable service to his team—

1, Proper way to leave feet in falling on ball from stride—right or left foot—not from both feet. 2, Proper way to fall on ball. Covering ball with body and arms. 3, Proper way to prepare for catch. Hands raised, body relaxed, and eyes on ball. 4, Proper way to catch. Arms forming sides of basket, body giving with ball.

PLATE III

1, Proper way to hold ball is very important. Unless ball is held as illustrated fumbling cannot be avoided. 2, The secondary defense, which is composed of the back-field men, never make a move until they are absolutely certain just where the ball has started for. 3, The forward pass is a very important factor in the new game. Every player should be instructed in the proper method of making a pass. The fingers along the lacing, hand carried back. The ball is shot forward by a short, snappy motion of the arm, as in base ball.

PLATE IV

since in no way can big gains be so quickly or easily made as through the kicking game. Therefore it is of the greatest importance that as many of the backs as possible should be good kickers, or at least punters.

Indeed a good kicking game, if successful, is certain to bring with it quicker and more frequent scoring than almost any other style of play. This is due, of course, to the enormous distances which good kicks cover, together with the consequent saving of time and energy. Even more attention should be devoted to catching, for almost nothing in foot ball may result so disastrously as a bad fumble in the back-field. Unless a back is sure at catching, or shows signs of becoming sure, with practice and experience, he should never be allowed to attempt catching. Bungling work in the back-field is the most demoralizing thing that can happen to any team.

Carrying the ball is the main function of the backs, hence the need of knowing how to carry it safely. This depends upon the way in which the ball is held. For end runs one end of the ball should be tucked under the arm—not too far under, so that it can be knocked out—while the other end should be firmly grasped and covered with the hand. In bucking, the ball should be held in the pocket formed by the stomach and legs, as the runner crouches, with both hands, though in case a back feels that he has the ball secure there is no reason why he should not use one hand to ward off opponents (see illustration 2 in Plate II). In the case of end runs the back should be prepared to ward off runners with either hand, changing the ball when necessary from one side to the other. And whether bucking or running, a back should never allow himself to loosen this hold on the ball, owing to the necessity of giving much attention to passing some particular opponent. The grip on the ball should be automatic and vise-like. Where a back is uncertain of his hold he may get good practice by bouncing a ball against a wall and then clapping it at once into position on the return.

It is of course necessary that the backs should tackle and interfere well. This means that they should both tackle and interfere low—the only difference between the two being that in case of a tackle the runner takes hold of his man, while in the interference he does all that the tackler does except take hold. A high tackler or interferer has no place behind the line, particularly in these days.

Finally, no back can be effective who does not start quickly. An offense which is so slow in reaching its object as to allow a concentration of opponents at that spot before the play hits is of course worthless. The attack must be quick and hard. For this reason the backs should constantly practice getting off quickly and getting up their maximum speed instantly. There are several ways of starting. Some backs stand in a crouching position, with one foot a little in the rear of the other, and with the knees turned well in. This enables them to start to the right or left or to the front without a moment's loss of time and with great initial power. Other backs assume a sprinting start. The sprint start position, with only one hand touching the ground, and that only sufficiently to steady the runner, is at the present time generally conceded to be the most effective. Both ways are good; in fact, any way is good that will enable a back to get off quickly and in any direction. The things to be avoided are a momentary straightening of the back at the instant of the start, and a short backward step. In case the latter step seems necessary the back should take his position with one foot back to begin with, thus making it unnecessary to take an additional one. There should be no backward motion of either foot.

In general, backs should exercise extreme care to prevent unevenness in starting. Starting too soon or too late is only productive of fumbles and off-side play, to say nothing of the upsetting influence which it produces throughout the team.

Along with his fundamentals, every back should spend considerable time in learning the rules of the game. This part of the work is often entirely neglected, and much to the detriment of the individual, for how can a man play a game well or intelligently when he does not even know the rules governing the game? It is an altogether too common sight to see teams let opportunities slip through ignorance of the rules; indeed, such ignorance has on more than one occasion actually cost a team its game, and such neglect has even existed in some of the larger university teams.

A foot ball player is frequently called upon most unexpectedly, to decide instantly upon some question of the game, and just as frequently his decision or lack of decision enables him either to do the right or the wrong thing and thus either secure an added advantage or else precipitate an added disadvantage upon his side.

Every back should be absolutely familiar with the distinctions between a "safety," a "touchback" and a "touchdown." He should know what constitutes a "fair catch," what is a violation of it, and so on throughout the rules, especially as to the new rules relating to forward pass and kick.

And after the rules have been mastered, a player should be told to make his play always, in case of doubt—and *then* refer to the officials—and under no consideration to stop because he hears a whistle blow or because he hears some one yelling for him to stop. A player can never make a mistake in carrying out this suggestion, and may, on some occasion, save himself a bad blunder through a misunderstanding.

OFFENSE.

The position of back is one of the most exhausting ones in all foot ball. At no other position is there so little opportunity for rest or let-up. It is go, go, all the time, first with the ball, then in the interference, then on defense. It is necessary, then, that a back should always be in the very best of condition, never overworked, always full of vigor and life. It is better to underwork a back than to overwork him.

Of the two half-backs on a team it is generally planned that one shall be a good end runner, the other a good plunger or bucker. Such an arrangement gives more all around possibilities to an eleven, particularly where there is an opportunity for broken field running.

On the offense the position of the backs will depend upon the style of game that is adopted. Sometimes they are played a full five yards behind the rush line, on other occasions they are played a scant three, while on still other occasions they form at even greater or less distance. The possibilities of formation are never ending, especially under the new rules allowing forward passing. When in position, and just previous to starting, the backs should take every precaution to prevent giving the direction of the play away by unconscious glances, movements or "leanings." It is also well for the back to save himself whenever he can from the nervous tension of prolonged waiting. Many backs subject themselves to some such strain by getting onto their toes several moments before the ball is to be put in play, or by not "letting up" at the call of "time." This may be avoided if the back will "key himself up" just at the last moment. But above all a back should be steady. He should never in all his play slow up for his interference, or even allow any other back to be slowed up by dilatoriness on his own part. He should start instantly and "dig"—never letting up an instant for anything. He should play with indomitable spirit. If he fails to gain the first try he should grit his teeth and *make* it gain the second.

In end running a back should be careful not to run too close to his interference when, in case the interference is upset, he is likely to fall over his protectors. Instead he should run with a little interval between himself and his interference, thus giving himself a chance to see where they are going and to take instant advantage of any upset. Where possible it is well for a back to run low so long as he can see where he is going, for by so doing he is likely to cause his opponents a moment's delay in locating him. When tackled he should aim to fall forward. To this end he should run with his body slanting forward, where it is exceedingly difficult for an opponent to overcome the combined power of gravity and the player's efforts. After falling, a back should never hold the ball out at arm's reach, as there is danger that it may be stolen from him, or that he may be penalized for crawling.

In bucking, one of the very important points to be kept in mind is that of keeping the eyes open. A back who closes his eyes as he makes his plunge is likely to fall flat on his face when an opening in the line presents itself suddenly where he had expected to find the passage choked. A back should never allow himself to hesitate or slow up as he strikes the line; he should strike it while at his maximum speed. A back may run high or low, according to circumstances, particularly so long as he keeps his feet—a most valuable quality. It is also wise for the back to take short steps, as in this way he is not so likely to find himself too much spread out where the footing is hardly firm and where it is almost impossible to get his feet under him in case of some sudden shove or push. The legs should accordingly be bent as the back strikes the line, because in this way he is able to exert much lifting power in case of need. The arms and hands should also be used to make progress. Many backs lose much of their effectiveness because they utilize only a portion of their power. The feet should ordinarily be kept on the ground, because only when they are there are they of much service. When, however, there is an imperative need of making a gain of a foot or so the back had best dive at the line—this being especially applicable to the full-back. Hurdling is now absolutely forbidden. When downed after a buck—or after any play, for that matter—a back should instantly straighten out so that there are no doubled up joints for succeeding players to fall upon.

In attempting line bucking the back should keep his chin close in to his neck, so as to prevent having his head twisted back over his shoulder, and he should also buck with the muscles of the neck held tense. This will tend to prevent bad wrenches of the neck and possibly injury to it. When in the midst of a line-bucking play which has resolved itself into a pushing contest between the two teams, the back should seek an outlet at the point of least resistance, usually to be found by feeling his way in different directions, and in general, a back should not raise his head until he has wholly cleared the secondary defense, as in this position it is very difficult for opponents to stop him, unless they have a clean chance for a tackle.

In case a back feels any doubt about the signal for a play, he should at once call out, "Signal." Otherwise collisions, fumbles and confusion will result. And no matter what a back thinks, he should invariably follow out the signal. The fault is not his if the play does not gain, but it is absolutely his fault if he does not go where he is directed. This rule should be absolute.

Another rule which should be invariably followed is that of never running back. It is a back's function to advance the ball, If he is unable to do so he should at least never lose ground.

If a back fumbles he should fall on the ball at once, never attempting to pick it up unless it bounces high. Attempting to pick up a fumbled ball is only making a bad matter worse. A back is responsible for the ball if it comes to him, and he should always remember that the possession of it is of the first importance.

It is the half-back's duty to afford proper protection to his kicker. He should be reliable in keeping any particular opponent who may be assigned to him out of a given play. He should put his entire strength into every play and should always have his "nose on the ball." He should follow it everywhere. Mr. Forbes has hit the nail on the head in this respect when he says: "A man's value to his team varies as the square of his distance from the ball."

In the midst of play, whether on the offense or defense, the backs should seek to encourage each other by a word, a touch or a look. Such simple though effective aids to thorough sympathy and harmony between them should never be overlooked. A hearty word of confidence spoken immediately after a bad fumble or other blunder will always cause the unfortunate player to put new life and determination into his work, while a bit of cutting sarcasm will drive him to anger or else dishearten him. When off the field a back should never allow himself to make unfavorable comments on any of his fellow players, unless indeed it be to the coach or captain. Nothing is so likely to spoil relations among players as criticism—offered behind the back. Certain annoyances should be borne for the sake of the team, even though they may be at times very exasperating. When a fellow back or fellow player is injured and confined to his bed nothing will so contribute to hearty relationship as frequent calls and anxious solicitation for recovery.

DEFENSE.

On the defense the backs and ends will have much to look after. Each has his particular station behind the line, with its primary and secondary responsibilities. Just what these positions are, whether far from the rush line, near to it or in it, must depend upon the style of game that is being played. Suffice it to say, however, that all styles are planned to the same end—to stop opposing plays.

As a rule the backs are so distributed as to most broadly cover the possible openings at which opponents are likely to or direct their plays or direct their forward passes. Consequently as the opponent's offense varies, so should the defense. Harvard has eleven different defense formations, with the center the keystone in each. Sometimes it seems well to attempt to meet opponents behind their own line, at other times to meet them at the line, and on other occasions still to meet them behind your own line. Again, a back is sometimes held responsible for a run around the opposite side of the line from that on which he is stationed, so that the various combinations of responsibilities, due to the tactics of any particular opponent, are never ending.

Ordinarily the backs are looked upon as forming a secondary line of defense. In such a case they must exercise great care not to get drawn into a play too quickly, and yet they should be equally careful not to wait too long before attacking the play. A back who waits too long is as bad as one who goes in too early. A happy medium is what should be aimed at, and it can be obtained only by constant practice and vigilant watchfulness. To exercise this vigilance the back must needs stand high enough to see where the play is going, and at the same time not be so high as to allow of being struck by an opponent while in an extended position. The instant a back sizes up a play he should get as soon as possible to the point of attack, watching carefully for trick plays, short kicks and forward passes all the while. A back will seldom be fooled by such plays if he will aways keep a close eye on straggling players, and remember that the ball, not the motion of any mass, indicates the point of attack. Once a back has decided to attempt to head off a runner or a play, at a certain point, he should get his eye on the man with the ball and keep it there, never losing sight of him, always keeping his position in the interference in mind and *never* allowing himself to attempt to see where he is going. That part of it will take care of itself. Such precautions as those just outlined will prevent most any back from being fooled as to the location of the ball—owing to a temporary relaxation of vigilance. And vigilance in these days of concealed methods and forward passing is exceedingly necessary. In attempting to stop end runs, and in fact in stopping any play, a back should never allow an opponent to hit him with his body; he should keep his opponent away with his arms. A back has no business to allow himself to get hit. In meeting heavy interference the back should either dive at the base of the head of the play, or in case he is too slow in getting there he should, if chance offers, seek to swing the head of the play to one side where the direct line of pressure is broken and where a momentary delay will give his own players a chance to down the runner before the opponents have a chance to reorganize. Many times one man can upset a play effectually, where had he tried to tackle one of the players he would have been thrown off or dragged along some distance further.

The question as to whether a back shall break through and attempt to tackle behind an opponent's line is a very difficult one to treat. Sometimes, where a back is strong on the defense and the opposing line is weak it is advisable. But where the opposing rush line is a strong one and particularly where it is stronger than your own it is certainly inadvisable. In such a case the backs should hold themselves as reserves rather than as of the rush line. Otherwise, in case an opponent clears your rush line, a long run is likely to follow.

In everything that they do, whether on offense or defense, the three backs should combine in every possible way with the quarter-back. The center rush, the three backs and the quarter-back should practice constantly together so as to get the purely mechanical work of their positions well ordered, and in a contest the three backs should keep the quarter-back constantly informed of weak places in the opposing defense, that he may profit by them when occasion demands. In a nutshell, all four backs should strive for mental, moral and physical team play both on and off the field.

BACK-FIELD WORK.

In the back-field, the main function of the backs is the handling of kicks and forward passes, and they are the most trying functions of all foot ball. To have to catch a ball while one's opponents are in many cases standing within arm's reach like so many wolves ready to take advantage of the slightest slip-up is bad enough, but when these conditions are augmented by the necessity of judging a high kick or pass in a gale of wind, they become well-nigh unbearable except to the coolest, most skillful and best drilled players. Such, however, is the trying position in which backs often find themselves on thirty or forty separate occasions in a single game. And worst of all they are severely censured where they fail of a clean record. A team can never know how much kicking or passing it is likely to meet in any game until the game is on, and it can never know when the winning or losing of a game may turn upon the safe handling of a single kick or pass. The possibilities of catastrophes are greater in the back-field than in any other branch of foot ball play, and so it is imperative that only the most reliable men should represent an eleven there. The backs, then, cannot be given too much practice in catching kicks or passes under every possible condition. They should practice with ends running down on them, with the wind against the kicker as well as with him, with a wet and dry ball. Furthermore, they should be given an opportunity to handle rolling, bouncing and twisting balls.

Under ordinary circumstances only one back is kept in the back-field. It is his duty to handle all unexpected kicks and passes and to tackle any runner that may get by the other ten players. He must be a sure catcher and tackler, and something of a kicker. This back may find himself on some occasion in the very trying position of being the only man between his goal and a fast opponent. When this is the case he must, as a general rule, depend upon his own initiative for his line of action. No one else can lay it out for him. There are, however, one or two points which any back will do well to keep in mind. It is always a good plan to try to force the runner to take that direction that will bring him nearest to the side line, where it may be possible either to corner him or to force him out of bounds. There is little sense in undertaking to tackle a runner who has the whole field to maneuver in, when you can reduce the field by two-thirds. Another point to be kept in mind is that of never running at full speed at a runner whom it is your intention to tackle, especially when he has an opportunity to side-step or dodge you. This side-stepping is the easiest thing imaginable where the tackler bears down on his victim at full speed. It is frequently illustrated when ends overrun a fullback, who by a simple side-step eludes them and makes a good run. Instead, the back should run fast toward his opponent until he gets within fifteen or twenty yards of him, when he should slow up and get ready to respond to dodging, which can only be done when the back has full control of his body. And he should exercise great care not to be fooled by some false motion on the part of the runner. This false motion is usually given with the upper part of the body, and can only be detected by keeping a close watch on the hips, which will always give away the real tendency of the body.

In case it may at some time seem advisable to utilize the defensive ability of the goal tender, as we may call him, on the rush line, and consequently to put another man back there in his place, a sure catcher should be chosen even if he is unable to do much at open field tackling. The reasoning here is that where a back is given one opportunity to prevent a touchdown by a decisive tackle in the open field—which is frequently missed by even the best players, owing to the tremendous speed of the runner—he is given twenty chances to catch the ball where any one catch, if missed, might mean a touchdown. Under these circumstances it is of course better to provide for the common play rather than for the emergency. The goal tend should keep a sharp lookout for trick plays and where possible keep his fellow players posted by calling out advice which his distance from the scrimmage may enable him to give.

The moment the opponents give evidence of an intention to kick, one or two of the other backs should at once drop back to reinforce the goal tend. Care must of course be taken that the evidence is genuine before they go clear back, but once they feel sure of this point they should run back at full speed, looking over their shoulders about every ten yards to prevent the kick from surprising them, or else to be ready for a return to the line in case of a fake. Backs frequently loaf back to their position. This is all wrong; they should be either on the line or way back of it, with as little time as possible wasted in getting into either position. The distance of these backs from the rush line and their relative positions in the back-field will depend upon circumstances. If the kicker is a good one and has the wind at his back they should of course play further back than if he is a poor kicker and has a stiff wind against him. The thing to be avoided is the danger of playing too far back. This is a very common fault among novices, who dread having the ball kicked over their heads and who, in order to prevent such a catastrophe, play so far back that it is impossible for them to catch more than three out of five of the shorter kicks, owing to the impossibility of getting under the ball. It is better policy to take one chance in fifty of having a kick go over one's head for the sake of catching the great majority of them than it is to prevent a kick over one's head at the expense of having to handle them on the bounce, where the opportunities for gaining ground after the catch are *nil.* A ball may be allowed to bounce, for it no longer puts the opponents on-side. This should only be done, however, when the back finds that the ball is coming very badly to him. As a rule they should all be caught on the fly, and if balls are bouncing it shows that the backs are not covering the ground in a thorough manner.

Once they are the proper distance behind the line the backs should spread out in such a way as best to cover the territory in which the ball is likely to fall. To this end they should not stand too near each other or too near the side line. If they stand too near together they will overlap much ground, and if they stand too near the side line they will enable themselves to catch many balls which go in touch and which there is no need of providing for, while at the same time they will be unable to cover much important ground within the field. The backs should play far enough apart so that they can concentrate at any given spot in time to be of assistance to each other either in catching or in the interference. In case a strong wind is blowing at the kicker's back one of the backs should play a little in rear of the others in order to provide for a possible misjudging or for fumbles. Under ordinary conditions one of the backs should play well in front of the others in order to be ready for short kicks or other tricks. In case one of the backs essays a fair catch the others should be on the watch for a fumble. The best way to get practice on these various points is to put two sets of backs, with center, at work kicking and catching. Then a competition may be encouraged with the result that all the players become interested, and in the endeavor to win the competition give each other the best practice possible.

Whenever possible it is well to have ends run down under the kicks, thereby giving the backs every opportunity to catch kicks "under fire." Continuous back-field practice is very exhausting, so that it is well whenever much practice of this kind is undertaken to have alternate squads of players, thereby saving all of them from overwork. Should the backs become tired of the practice and allow it to become lackadaisical, it should at once be discontinued, as carelessness in back-field practice is worse than none at all.

In preparing to catch kicks the backs should make every endeavor to get under the ball in time enough to enable them to receive it while they are standing still. To do this they must be able to "size up" a ball as soon as it rises in the air.

In running up on a ball the backs should also be careful not to overrun it, remembering that it is much easier to run up on a ball than to run back for it in case it is misjudged. Furthermore, in case a back who is careful to keep the ball in front of him misjudges it and it hits him in the chest, he stands a much better chance of recovering the ball as it falls in front of him than he would have if he overran the ball and it fell behind him.

While in the act of catching, a back should concentrate his entire attention on the ball, never attempting to divide it with the opposing ends. The plea that a back often advances for this tendency is that he is afraid of a bad fall just as he is completing the catch, or that he wants to see where the ends are, that he may dodge them more effectively, etc., etc. These excuses should all be denied on the ground that the possession of the ball is *the* thing. And in this connection it is just as well to say that in case a back fumbles in the back-field he should fall on the ball at once. This point should be so drilled into the players that it will become second nature to them.

The moment a back has caught the ball he should turn his attention to his opponents, seeking how he can dodge them and run the kick back. In case he catches the kick in time to decide from his own observations in which direction to run, a back should experience little difficulty in getting off safely. But when the ball and the ends arrive almost simultaneously the situation is more difficult. In such a position the other backs should assist by a word or two. At first the giving of such directions will end in much confusion, but as the backs become more and more accustomed to each other this difficulty will disappear, to be followed by satisfactory results. Where a back is a good dodger he can often fool opponents by making a false start in one direction and then following it up with a real start in another. This ability is natural, and no coaching can develop it except where the player has in him the crude qualities.

One thing, however, every back can be taught, and that is that he shall never run back. Running back in back-field work is even more fatal than in ordinary scrimmage play. Another thing to be borne in mind is that under no circumstances can a back use his "straight-arm" more effectually than in the broken field running that forms such a big part of back-field work.

How to Play Quarter-back

BY WALTER H. ECKERSALL,

University of Chicago; All-America Quarter-back, 1905 and 1906.

The position of quarter-back is considered by many to be the most important one on a foot ball team, but to my mind each of the eleven positions is a critical one. At some time during every game an opportunity comes to each man to play his position as it should be played, and on his ability to grasp that opportunity depends the result of many a contest.

A foot ball team is composed of eleven men, and if, as sometimes happens, one man is apparently doing all the scoring, you may be sure the other ten men are doing their duty in order to make such a feat possible, and praise should be given to them equally with the fortunate individual performer.

The quarter-back position may wisely be termed the keystone one of a team. Especially is this so, as is usually the case, when the quarter-back gives the signals. He is then truly the field captain and largely responsible for the outcome of the contest through which he directs his men.

A team should have the utmost confidence in its quarter-back in order to play with the speed and precision by which games are won. On the other hand, the quarter-back, by steady, consistent play and ability to deal with emergencies should merit this confidence. Often the very tones in which the signals are given can bring order out of chaos, and vice versa.

There are just as many different ways of playing quarter-back as there are coaches and quarter-backs. Of course, a certain set of playing rules must be followed, but aside from that, the field left for devising original plays is large and on the coach largely depends the origin of these plays. If the formations are such that a great deal of time is required to carry them out successfully the playing of the quarter-back will naturally be slower, and, on the other hand, if trick playing, running and kicking are resorted to, the speed of the quarter-back is proportionately increased.

The material with which a coach has to work often determines the style of play to be adopted. If the men are heavy, and consequently slow, the plan of action will have to be along the line of their plunging, line-plugging abilities. And, on the other hand, if the material is light, a speedy, crafty campaign must be planned to offset the lack of weight.

Other points which the coach considers carefully in devising the plays for his quarter-back are the abilities and handicaps of the opposing team. Perhaps one team is noted for a certain style of play, hence plays are planned to cope successfully, if possible, with this method. These plans failing, often an entirely different mode of procedure is expounded to the players between the halves by the coach, and the quarter-back receives his instructions accordingly.

As each succeeding team naturally puts up a different game the coach is obliged to think up new plays constantly and teach them to his men.

So it seems to me the coach does a great deal of hard work that the quarter-back is generally given credit for. Still, the quarter-back must use his good judgment in the direction of these plays in the heat of battle, or the best-laid plans of the coach are for naught; so, perhaps, after all the responsibility is equally divided.

REQUIREMENTS OF THE QUARTER-BACK.

As a general rule, with but few exceptions, the quarter-back is a small fellow, weighing in the neighborhood of one hundred and fifty pounds, small of stature but very compactly built, a good runner, plenty of nerve, good judgment and cool-headed.

The new rules promise to add to the requirements of their positions, especially in ability to run, and all the backs are liable to be quarter-backs.

Theoretically, he is the captain of the team, for he directs its play from the start of the game to the end. If he is an intelligent and experienced player, his judgment will rarely be questioned by the captain, and if this be the case the captain should be reprimanded for such interference. The quarter-back is depended upon for the team's victories and blamed, generally, for its defeats.

This man should have a combination of qualities, which, fortunately, most quarter-backs have.

First—He must have a good memory. He should be able to remember from sixty to seventy different plays and the signals for them, and he must know them in such a way that there is no hesitancy or delay on his part in giving them.

Second—He must be able to devise some plan for finding out the weaknesses in the opposing team, and then hammer them consistently. This is accomplished most readily by using the full-back and sending him at every point in the line, thus finding some spot which is weaker than any of the others.

Third—He must not use any man too much, for fear of tiring him too quickly, thus weakening the offense and the team as a result.

Fourth—He should consult with his own line men in regard to the position of their opponents, thus ascertaining, in a measure, the chances of sending a play through one of them with a marked degree of success.

Fifth—He should always encourage his teammates, whether they are being outplayed or otherwise, for it is too well known in foot ball that the players never lie down and a little encouragement goes a great way.

Sixth—He must always bear in mind the coach's instructions, and also consider them seriously.

Seventh—Always consider your opponents as gentlemen.

Eighth—Always treat the officials in a courteous manner, being ever mindful of the fact that they are selected as impartial overseers of the game, and, too, that any act of discourtesy on the part of any player gives the officials the power to send the offender from the game.

Ninth—Be a cheerful loser and give the credit where it belongs.

Tenth—Take your victories modestly and your defeats with courage.

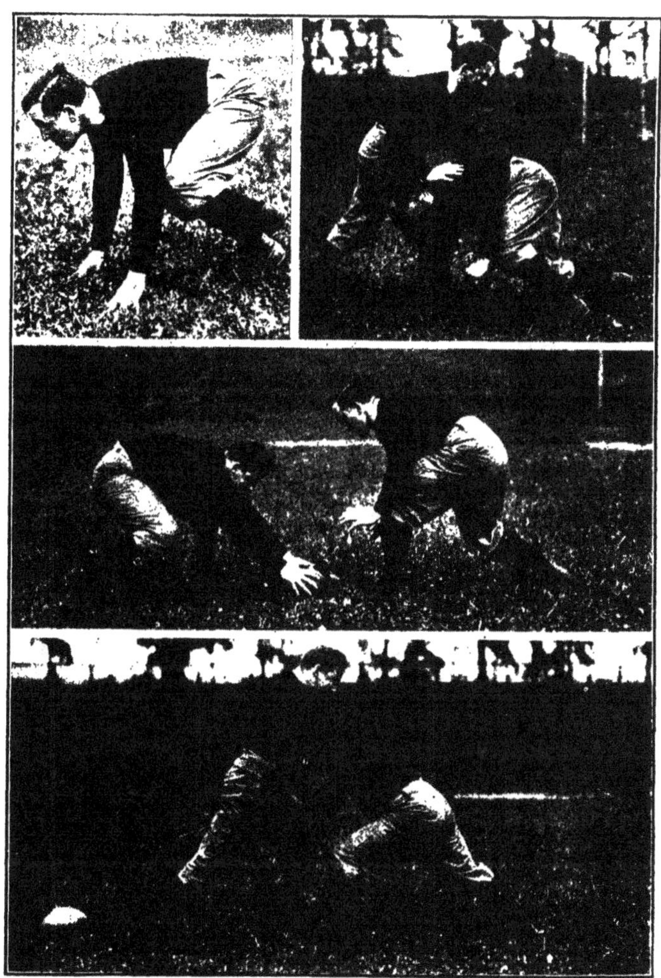

1, Proper way for back-field men to start when on offense. A "sprinter's start." 2, Proper method for line men to employ in charging opponents. After taking position for a quick start, charge with ball, throwing shoulder into opponent and carry him back out of the play. 3, Proper method for line men to employ in charging. Feet well braced, hands extended and eyes on ball, ready for the charge. 4, Improper method for line men to employ in blocking opponents. No strength to charge on account of position of feet and body.

PLATE V

1, Quarter-back stands in back and under center, hand open, with center passing ball directly into extended hand. 2, Proper way for quarter-back to make pass to half-back on line buck. 3, Proper way to make forward pass. Ball carried back to rear of head, eyes looking for free man, hand extended forward to ward off opponents. 4, Proper way to place ball for run in open. Ball should be placed under the outside arm, one apex being held snugly by arm and body and the other by the hand of the same arm. 5, Proper way for half-back to receive ball on direct pass for run around end, or on a forward pass. Ball should be caught close to body.

PLATE VI

POSITION OF THE QUARTER-BACK.

There will be many new positions for the back-field men, but in regular formation the quarter-back should stand squarely behind the center in a crouched position. It is necessary that he holds his hands in a fixed position to receive the ball. He should make no move whatever, with his hands, or by a dip, from bending of the knees, to receive the ball, for if he does he immediately gives a warning to the opposing team, thus enabling them in many cases to get the charge on his own teammates. In connection with this, it may be necessary to add, that it is very helpful to have a starting signal. This enables the team to start at the same time and does not give the opponents any undue advantage, which might come if the quarter were to give a motion with his hands or some other outward sign.

In receiving the ball from the center, the quarter should use his hands as much as possible. I have found it very useful by having my hands close to my body in such a manner that the ball comes in contact with my body and hands at practically the same time, causing no delay whatever, in passing the ball to the player who was called upon to carry it on that particular play.

Many coaches advocate a side position, which necessitates, as they claim, a surer pass from the center, but it does not allow the quarter to start quickly, thus delaying him in getting the ball to the runner immediately, which is a very essential point.

The quarter must familiarize himself as much as possible with the ball. He should spend plenty of time working with his center, making whatever adjustments and suggestions he deems necessary for the further perfection of his play. He must spend some time practising with a wet, heavy ball, for no one can tell when the conditions will be such that the ball will become wet, heavy and soggy.

PASSING.

In my estimation, passing is the most important work of the quarter-back. As has already been stated, nearly every team has its quarter coached differently in the various branches of attack. When the full-back is called upon to make a straight plunge on the half-back for a straight buck or cross-buck the quarter should *never* fail to place the ball in the stomach of the man who is to carry it (see illustration 2 in Plate VI). This is a cardinal point in the work of the quarter and too much emphasis cannot be laid on it.

If the full-back is to make a straight buck on the right of center, the quarter should pivot on his left foot, quarter of the way round, and with his left hand *place* the ball in the pit of the stomach of the full-back, and vice versa if he bucks on the left side. The same theory holds true in passing to the half-backs for straight bucks and cross-bucks, only on the cross-bucks he steps to the side and back, and places the ball in the stomach as before. Of course, in the wide end runs and trick plays this cannot be carried out, but should be always borne in mind by the quarter-back.

This point of passing is very essential to good team work, for nothing will slow up a team quicker than poor passing, which is of course the fault of the quarter-back. If the players begin to lose confidence in the quarter-back they will not put the same dash and drive in their work as they would otherwise. Then again, the quarter-back is only a cog in the great machine, and he should fulfill his part of the work without any hesitation or delay.

TACKLING.

As a general rule the offensive quarter-back plays defensive full-back on defense and as such innumerable opportunities present themselves for him to test his own tackling ability.

When playing the above position on defense it is best to play from fifteen to twenty yards back of the scrimmage, thus enabling the quarter to stop a runner in the open field without any considerable gain, and because it is easier to stop him then than it would be if he once obtained a good start.

Too much time cannot be spent in practising tackling. It is a fundamental requisite of his position and should be perfected by him, more than by any one else.

The quarter should *never* run up on a man, when he once gets loose, for it is the easiest thing in the world to dodge a man when he is coming up to meet you. The tackler must wait for the runner to come to him, and then by some original schemes, such as a little jumping sideways, endeavor to hit him about the thighs, as the rule forbidding tackling below the knees is strictly enforced. The quarter must be able to tackle with both shoulders equally well, and should not favor one shoulder, as is quite frequently the case.

It is generally better to corner the runner, if possible, between the side-line and yourself, and when you are absolutely sure you have him safe, you should make a running dive at him, thus enabling the tackler to break any stiff-arm and prevent the runner from dodging. Nothing is more distasteful to the follower of foot ball than to see a half-hearted attempt at tackling, such as a tackle around the neck or by the arm. From such attempts as these injuries are inflicted, occasionally of a serious nature.

The defensive quarter of course is forced by circumstances to tackle a runner wherever he can. The player in this position should be a man of experience, intelligence and strength. He should be able to size up situations quickly and direct his team-mates accordingly. An experienced, defensive quarter is occasionally able to foresee a certain play by the actions of the backs of the opposing team. Not infrequently does an experienced half or full-back point with his eyes or feet in the direction of a play and naturally more so in the case of the inexperienced player. One great point, which he must continually bear in mind, is not to go into a play too quickly, for it may happen that it is a fake or split interference play, and, naturally, to get the defensive quarter drawn in, adds to the value of the play. He must always throw himself under a pile and never try to resist a mass standing up.

As a general rule the play on a fourth down is either a kick or a buck through the line, and after the game is fifteen minutes old the man backing up the line should know what is going to happen.

INTERFERENCE.

The quarter-back is quite an important man in the interference and much can be said about his work in this particular branch. In straight plunges by the halves or full-back, he should *not* attempt to get in ahead of the runner. The quicker the play gets up to the line of scrimmage, the more value it has. When the quarter plays thus he is practically a free man and must be constantly alert for fumbles, which occasionally happen and frequently result seriously. In end-running, it is a cardinal principle for the quarter to head the interference.

In open-field interference the interferer should not hesitate to leave his feet to take a man out of the way, especially if the opponent is the defensive full-back. Of course, the interferer must make sure of his man, and this can best be done by getting him between the side-line and himself, then making a lunge for him, so that his body will strike the tackler about the knees. But the interferer must be certain of his position before the lunge is made, as the tackler may side-step the interferer as he takes the lunge. This is the surest way there is for taking a man out of the way, and it is a form that *can* be accomplished with practice. Work on the tackling dummy is mighty good for this.

HANDLING PUNTS.

No one rule can be laid down telling a player how to catch a foot ball, but numerous suggestions can be made upon this point.

A punted ball has no definite direction, for it may be diverted from its course by numerous air currents which come from openings in the grandstands or other sources, thus making it very hard to judge the ball accurately. Of course the ball is caught against the body, if properly judged, with the aid of the arms and hands. It is also a good thing to bring the leg in action, by pulling it up in such a manner as not to allow the ball to drop downward after being caught.

The quarter-back should pay no attention whatever to the men who are coming down to tackle him. He *must* make sure of the ball and then of the men.

When he has caught the ball he should carry it in such a way that the point is well up under the arm and the other point resting in the palm of his hand. When he is tackled he must be absolutely sure to hold on to the ball by wrapping both arms around it. It is a rather poor policy to attempt to catch a ball on the run, as the chances of missing it are greater than the chances of catching it. When carrying the ball the runner should *never* run straight into a man, because an injury is easier averted by side-stepping and getting the force of the blow on the side.

Kick-offs are different from punts in that they have a definite direction, thus making them easier to catch. It is best to catch kick-offs on the run, if possible, because they are much simpler to handle and the catcher runs very little risk of dropping them, and then, again, he is moving rather fast, covering the ground and in a better position to dodge. Always get possession of the ball if it goes behind the goal line, for if the opponents get it, it is a touchdown for them.

GIVING SIGNALS.

The quarter-back in giving signals must give them loud and clear. The fundamental point in this branch of the quarter's work is his utmost familiarity with the signals. He must have them continually at his tongue's end and he should help other members of the team memorize them.

If a signal is to be repeated the quarter must rise from a crouching to a standing position and give the signal with the same clearness and distinctness as before. He must never turn to either side and repeat the signal, for he may unconsciously give the play away. When a repetition of the signal is called for it is best to turn around and face the backs and then turn back and give it to the line. Especially is this true on a day when there is plenty of noise, and for this reason I favor series plays, when two or three plays can be run off from one signal, thus giving a team the advantage of fast play.

PUNTING AND DROP-KICKING.

It is a rather difficult matter to describe how to kick a foot ball accurately. Kicking applies to punting as well as scoring from the field, but the two branches of this part of the game are absolutely distinct.

It is hardly necessary, I suppose, to explain that a punt differs from a drop-kick in that when the former is made the ball is dropped and kicked before it touches the ground. In a drop-kick the ball is dropped to the ground and kicked just as it is rising on the bound.

In the last few years, with the development of place-kicking, drop-kicking has to a certain extent gone out of use. So far as I am concerned I prefer drop-kicking to place-kicking. In the latter form of scoring the responsibility is divided between two men—the one who holds the ball and the actual kicker. This division of responsibility of course doubles the chances of failure, for not only must the kicker do his work accurately and quickly, but the man who holds the ball also must make no mistake.

Just what is the exact secret of successful kicking is as hard for me to explain as for any one else. No two kickers use absolutely the same method. I know that when I was first learning to kick I was frequently told by good coaches that my method was all wrong.

The two most important points about kicking, whether it is punting or drop-kicking, are accuracy and speed. No matter how good a kicker a man may be—no matter how accurate even—if he is not fast in getting the ball away he is practically helpless. Therefore, a man learning to kick should endeavor first and foremost to attain speed. The kind that is best understood by the phrase, "Make haste slowly."

The kicker should always try to make a kick in just the same space of time, whether he is merely practising on a clear field or actually kicking from behind the line in a game. He should try and feel just as if there were no one trying to break through the line and block his kick. He should know he has just about so many seconds in which to get the ball away and he must take all that time to increase the accuracy of the kick.

Accuracy, after a certain point in the development of kicking, is better than distance. An accurate punter can generally place the ball so that a man on the opposing team who catches it is almost sure to be tackled before he can run back any great distance. On the other hand, as one frequently sees in a game, some punter gets great distance, but the man who catches the ball is able to run it back.

In punting, the kicker should always have a good idea of just where the opposing back-field men are waiting to receive the ball. It should be his idea to get the greatest possible distance, at the same time trying to put the ball where it is hardest for the opponent to get it and where the ends on his own team will have the least difficulty in making a tackle.

All this applies to punting, but although this is the most important branch in the kicking end of the game, it is the drop-kicking that appeals to the spectator. A large proportion of every crowd at a game knows really little about the finer points of foot ball. This class of spectators does not realize how important punting is. A man is apt to forget that a single punt may gain forty or fifty yards in a few seconds, which it has taken the opposing team many minutes of hard play to obtain.

This is not the case with drop-kicking. If the drop-kick is successful, it gains three points, and the spectators appreciate it more than any other kind of kicking, just as they are apt to think more of the effort which gains the last yard for a touchdown than of a much longer gain made earlier.

As I have already said, it is rather hard to explain how to make drop-kicks. In making such a kick the kicker should get the ball on a high pass, about shoulder high, then turn a little to the right before dropping the ball to the ground Then just as it rises on the bound he is in a position to swing at it with his right leg full force.

Foot Ball Generalship

By Glenn S. Warner,
Head Foot Ball Coach at the University of Pittsburgh; formerly Athletic Director at the Carlisle Indian School.

The following chapter on "Foot Ball Generalship" has been reprinted by permission of Mr. Warner from his book, "Foot Ball for Players and Coaches" (Copyright, 1912, by Glenn S. Warner).

Under this head it is intended to treat, not only of the generalship with which an important game should be handled, but of the intelligent management of the whole season's campaign.

THE SCHEDULE.

The schedule is generally arranged with the idea of providing the team with practice games early in the season, these games increasing in importance as the season progresses, and leading up to one or two final championship games which are made the climax of the season, and for which nearly every other game is considered as a means of development and preparation.

The strongest teams, as a rule, try to arrange their schedules so that the games will be comparatively easy at the start, and harder as the season advances, but with the idea of reaching the final championship game or games without a defeat. The weaker teams very often arrange their early games with stronger teams out of their class, realizing that they will almost surely be beaten, but with the idea of giving the players practice and experience which will aid them later in the season in their championship games with teams in their own class.

Occasionally a supposedly minor team will be blessed with unusually good material; which will get together early, and by developing quickly, try to surprise a so-called "big" team which has scheduled an early practice game with them. If the minor team happens to win such a game, it gives the players some temporary glory and notoriety, but usually results in disaster before the end of the season, by reason of overconfidence or "swelled head," and overtraining because of getting into top-notch condition too soon. While it is a laudable desire for every team to win all the games possible, the success of the season will usually be greater if the early games are considered as practice games pure and simple, and no special preparation made for them. The games later in the season are usually the ones upon which the standing of the team, or the success of the season, is based, and these should be the contests to be borne in mind throughout the season, and gradually worked up to. In doing this, the other games should not be overlooked by any means, nor played without putting forth every effort, and making such careful preparation as will not interfere with the steady and gradual development of the team.

Some schedules are arranged in such a manner that a very important game has to be played in the middle of the season and another at the end. With such a schedule, the team is usually developed rather early, and put in prime condition for the midseason game, after which it is easily handled for a week or two, and then developed for the second, or final climax. A team which has a schedule arranged in this manner will very seldom play in top-notch form in both of these games, and unless it is an unusually strong one, is almost sure to be beaten in one of them. With a schedule like this, it will prove to be good generalship to regard the final game as the most important, and not have the team in top-notch form for the midseason contest. It will be wise to follow both suggestions, because if the midseason game should be won without being in top-notch form, but with the idea that it was of more importance than the final contest, overconfidence and lack of interest would then ruin the team's chances in the latter.

About the poorest schedule a team can have is one in which the most important game comes about the middle of the season, and closing with a game of minor importance. A team with such an arrangement of games may do well in the early season, and in its important game, but is almost sure to deteriorate and spoil its reputation in the latter part of the season, by reason of overconfidence, and lack of interest and enthusiasm.

No matter how the schedule is arranged, it should be the aim of every team to make gradual and steady improvement as the season progresses. If defeats come, everything possible should be done to keep the players from becoming disheartened, and the defects in the team's play which caused the defeats should be pointed out to the players and corrected. No schedule should be arranged which will necessitate playing more than half the games with teams known to be stronger than the team for which it is arranged, because nothing will so dishearten the players as several successive defeats. One or two defeats, early or in the middle of the season, usually aid in developing a team, because they bring out the weak points and keep the players in a receptive mood for coaching. It is just as great a mistake to arrange a schedule which is too easy as it is to make it too hard. If the practice games, leading to the final game or games, are all with teams of a minor class and easily won, the championship games will be reached without having had a chance to properly test the players or the plays. Some players will appear to excellent advantage in the minor games, but will be found wanting when up against strong opponents, and many plays, which work well against weaker teams, will be found worthless in games where the teams are evenly matched; therefore every team should have some games with worthy opponents before their championship games are reached, in order that the faint-hearted or easily rattled players and the unsuccessful plays may be weeded out.

THE MATERIAL.

Good judgment, or generalship, should be exercised in handling the material and in placing the players in the positions for which they are best fitted. No matter how good the backs may be, they cannot accomplish much behind a weak line, while mediocre backs will be able to get good results behind a strong line; therefore it is of first importance to so arrange the players as to provide a strong line. As a rule, it will be found that the inexperienced candidates, provided they have sufficient weight, will be able to do better work as guards, or at center, than in any other positions, because experience and knowledge of the game are not so necessary for the three center men. A player who has had considerable experience as a guard can easily learn to play tackle; and as a rule, a player who has learned to play tackle can be developed into a good end, provided he has enough of speed; therefore a good rule to follow, in arranging the players in the line, is to place the inexperienced men in the three center positions, and move out the experienced ones, placing those with the greatest experience and most ability at the ends.

In choosing a quarter-back the liveliest, coolest and headiest player among the candidates should be picked out, whether he has had experience in playing the position or not. Such a player will easily learn the duties of a quarter-back and be able to render better service here than anywhere else upon the team. Without a quarter-back who is a general and a leader, in whom the other players have the utmost confidence, no team will be able to get satisfactory results.

The heaviest of the back-field material should, as a rule, be placed in the position of full-back, and in selecting all of the backs, their defensive ability should be considered just as important as their ability to advance the ball. Every team should have at least two good punters and a field goal kicker in its makeup, although these need not necessarily be backs.

Left-handed and left-footed players are better suited to positions upon the right side of the line than upon the left.

The man who has the handling and the selection of the material in charge must be a general, as he has all kinds of temperaments to deal with and will be confronted with many situations and difficulties, which must be handled with tact and diplomacy. He must show no favoritism, and should endeavor, by all means, to keep the players in good humor, and free from jealousies and ill-feeling toward each other. Harmony should be the watchword of the season, because no combination of individuals working together for a common purpose can secure the best results unless they pull together, and this is especially true of a foot ball team.

PLANNING THE CAMPAIGN.

In preparing for all except the early practice games, a study should be made of the systems of offense and defense relied upon by the opponents, so that the players may be instructed as to the best method of meeting them. The plays may have to be changed slightly from week to week, in order to cope with different styles of defense, while the formations and plays relied upon by opposing teams will necessitate changes in the regular system of defense. It is a good plan to have the scrub or second team play as nearly as possible the same style of game in the practice games of the week that will be used by the team which will be met on Saturday

Having learned how to meet different systems or styles of play as the season progresses, the players will be ready to meet most any situation in the final games, and not be rendered helpless by having something new sprung upon them.

A special study should be made of the style of game played by the team or teams with whom the championship games are to be played and the whole season should be centered upon these games. While the other games should be prepared for and played with determination and spirit, they should be regarded as of minor importance, and every effort put forth to instill in the players the importance of the championship game or games, and an intense desire and determination to fairly overcome their rivals.

The mental attitude of the players toward the opponents or the games plays a very important part in the result of many games. No team will do its best if the players go into a game without a full realization that they will have to put forth their best efforts to win or are overconfident; and very often under such conditions the unlooked-for strength and determination of the opponents will so surprise, daze and demoralize a team that the game results in a disastrous defeat, which might have been avoided if the players had gone into the game with the right spirit.

THE GAME.

During the week preceding a championship game the team should be handled very carefully. If there are any players suffering from injuries, they should not engage in any rough exercise, and the practice of the week should be devoted to smoothing up the plays and perfecting the team work.

If the game is to be played away from home, but within a two or three hours' ride, the trip will interfere less with the players if taken upon the morning of the day of the game than if taken the day before, because the players will rest better in their own beds, and will not be so affected by nervous excitement as they would be in a strange place, near the scene of the struggle. Where the game is to be played more than a hundred miles from home, the trip should be made the day before and, if possible, arranged so that the destination will be reached during the afternoon or evening. The journey, if not too long, will just tire the players enough to make them sleep well. It is not a good plan to make the trip to the place where the game is to be played two or three days ahead, as the excitement prevailing in the locality and the change of surroundings and food are likely to have an injurious effect upon the players.

The team should be prepared with an outfit suitable for any kind of weather conditions, especial attention being given to the shoes and the cleats upon them. If the field is muddy, or if it is rainy, the suits should be light and the cleats upon the shoes long. If the weather is very cold, it will be advantageous for the players to wear warm underwear.

Before tossing for the choice of the goal or the kick-off, the direction of the wind and the position of the sun should be noted, and also the tendency of the wind to increase or diminish late in the afternoon. In some localities the wind diminishes as night approaches, and in this case the winner of the toss should choose the goal favored by the wind; whereas, if the wind is likely to increase toward evening, the choice should be made so as to get the benefit of the wind in the last period.

When a team receives the kick-off with a favored wind, or a wind blowing across the field, good generalship on the part of the opposing team should cause it to place the kick-off to the side or corner of the field least favored, or to the windward side. If successful in so placing the kick, the team receiving it (provided it is run back straight ahead from the point where the ball is caught) will be forced, when it punts, to kick the ball across the path of the wind to keep it from going out of bounds; while if the ball was kicked off to the other side, the ball could be returned by a punt diagonally across the field with the wind almost behind it. It is usually good generalship, in any case, for the kick-off to be placed to the side because the best man to run the ball back is usually placed directly in front of the goal, and it is wise to kick the ball where he cannot get it. It is also more difficult for the receiving team to get together and form interference at one side of the field than in the center, and the team kicking off can place its best tacklers and an extra man or two upon the side toward which the kick-off is to be made.

A foot ball game is very similar, in many respects, to a war, and good generalship is as important in one as in the other. Each scrimmage represents a battle, in which the opposing forces are lined up opposite each other, one side defending itself against the attack of the other. The lines represent the infantry, and the backs can be likened to cavalry, quick moving, and able to charge the enemy at any spot or rush to the support of any position attacked. The quarter-back or general of the side making the attack should study well the defense of the enemy, and decide whether to force through their center, turn their flank by a quick movement, deceive them with a fake movement in one direction while the real attack is made at another spot, or transfer the battle to a more favorable locality by a punt. In making this decision, he should take into consideration the condition of the field, the direction of the wind, and especially the position on the field, with reference to the goal or side lines, and the number of the down and the distance to be gained. If the wind is favorable, and the ball is near the goal line which his team is defending, the battle should by all means be transferred to the enemy's territory by a punt, reserving ammunition and strength for the attack when an opportunity is gained within striking distance of the enemy's goal.

As a rule the ball should be punted out of a team's territory unless there is an adverse wind, in which case it is usually better to retain the ball until forced to punt. Upon fourth down, unless near the opponents' goal, the ball should be punted or forward passed when there is not a reasonable certainty that the required distance for a first down can be gained, and this should amount to almost absolute certainty where the team in possession of the ball is in its own territory.

If a team is able to hold the opponents and prevent their gaining, it is wise to punt often, especially if the team excels in a punting game; but where the opponents are the stronger, and able to make consistent gains when rushing the ball, the weaker team should retain the ball as long as possible whenever they gain possession of it, and only punt when forced to do so upon fourth down, because so long as the ball is kept away from their opponents, the latter are unable to make much headway or score. Such tactics are also advisable when a team has a lead and is content to keep the other side from overtaking them, as it is very discouraging for a losing team, only a few points behind, to realize that the time is fast slipping away, and that they may be unable to get a chance to use their plays and score before the whistle blows.

When rushing the ball, the quarter should choose one of the strongest plays for use upon the first down—one which is usually good for five or more yards, and generally such plays should be directed outside of tackle. If the defense of the opponents is scattered, it may be advisable to send the first play through the line, but usually it is not wise to depend upon gaining ten yards in four downs by bucking the line. If four or more yards are gained upon the first trial, the remaining distance necessary for a first down can usually be secured by straight plays which can be depended upon for steady and sure gains. If the play used upon first down is unsuccessful, an end run or a trick play should be used upon the second down, and if this is stopped without much gain, a forward pass, trick play or a strong play outside of tackle should be resorted to upon the third down.

On fourth down, unless practically certain of gaining the required distance, the ball should be punted unless it is near enough to the opponent's goal for a field goal trial. A forward pass would be the proper play on fourth down near the opponent's goal and on the side of the field where a field goal would be difficult.

Good generalship is as necessary upon the part of the players, and especially upon the part of the captain, when the team is upon the defense, as when rushing the ball. By studying the situation upon every down, noting the distance to be gained and the part of the gridiron where the ball is situated, the defensive players can determine pretty closely what sort of tactics will be used upon nearly every play. The backs particularly should be able to size up what play to be on the lookout for and change their positions accordingly, closing in when expecting a line attack and moving back when a punt, a forward pass or a trick play is likely to be pulled off. If the field and the ball are slippery, the defense should play in much closer than upon a dry day, because end runs and fancy plays will be impossible under these conditions, and the main strength of the attack will very likely consist of plays directed at the line.

All the defects in the team's play can be noted during the first period and corrected during the intermission, and the team which is in the hands of the best general, whether he be captain or coach, will usually show the greatest improvement as the game progresses.

1, Back-field men should "pick-off" opposing ends by throwing their bodies or legs into opponents. 2, "Pick-off" interference is something that all line men should excel at. 3, "Blocking kicks" is a requirement that is second to none. Picture illustrates kick after it was blocked. The right hand extended to block, left hand and arm used to protect face. 4, Many successful runs have been made from fake forward passes. The back "fakes" a pass, opponents hesitate and endeavor to perfect a secondary defense; in meantime back carrying ball sifts through open defense of opponents for a substantial gain.

PLATE VII

1, Position of center on offense. Feet well apart, ball forward and body in such a position that each and every muscle is under self-control. 2, Position of center and guard on offense. Guard well up on line of scrimmage, eyes on ball and body in such a position that a quick start is obtainable. 3, Position of center and guard in kick formation. Guard "locking" inside leg with that of center. 4, Position of guard and tackle on defense. On defense, line men spread out from one and one-half to two yards apart. 5, Position of guard and tackle on offense. Tackle close to guard, making inside of himself safe.

PLATE VIII

How to Coach a Prep School Team

By Ed Thorp.

Coaching a squad of prep school footballers is a far different proposition than that of instructing a team of collegians. In the first place, the extreme youth of the schoolboy, as well as his lack of the necessary weight to play the game properly, are two of the setbacks that confront the school rather than the 'varsity coach. Second, the rawness of the material is another obstacle that the school coach must overcome, if a winning combination is to be developed. All of the above problems should be solved long before the actual coaching of the candidates is even thought of.

The man who assumes the responsibilities of coach must, therefore, have a fair knowledge of the kind of material that he is going to have and then decide upon some practical plan of development. A systematic plan of attack, as well as one for the defense, are absolutely necessary.

After arriving at a decision as to a plan of development, a suitable field for practice should be found. The field should be in close proximity to the school and be one that is of soft turf, rather than hard clay where the grass has long since worn off. Goal posts and cross bars should be erected according to the regulations of the game, at both extremities of the field. It is not absolutely necessary for the practice field to be of the regulation size, as specified in the book of rules. Of course, if it is possible to attain one of the proper dimensions, so much the better.

The next duty of the coach, one that calls for his undivided attention, is the supervision of the proper equipment for the various candidates. Too much time, labor or expense cannot be expended by either player or coach in seeing that each candidate procures the necessary clothes, as many players have been lost to a team by their neglect to properly protect themselves from injury during the first days of practice. A little saving of time and expense at the start of foot ball very often results in serious loss before the season's work has been completed.

Proper speed cannot be developed in a player if he wears a No. 9 shoe on a No. 5 foot. Good, tight fitting shoes, properly cleated, will contribute more to the speed of a team than anything else that I know of. Light, snug fitting pants, with guards at the hips, knees and thighs should be worn. Close fitting jerseys, as well as properly adjusted stockings, headgears and pads for the shoulders and elbows all go to make up the proper costume for foot ball players.

After all candidates have been clothed as described, special time for daily practice should be decided upon, and the coach would do well to impress upon all candidates at the start of the season that prompt and consistent attendance at daily practice, unless excused by injury or some other good cause, is the first and foremost requirement of foot ball players.

When all of the above have been taken care of in a proper and business like manner, a short instruction should be given to the candidates in the correct rules of training. All smoking, drinking, either of intoxicating liquors or sweet sodas, eating of pie, cakes or sweets, as well as late hours for retiring, should be things that a foot ball player must refrain from if perfect condition is to be obtained. Any breach of the above rules should be dealt with in no light manner, or else strict discipline among the candidates will be an impossibility.

The first day of actual practice should consist in a short drill in the proper way to catch, pass or receive the ball. A small amount of running should be indulged in by all, but a strict eye should be kept on the players to see that none overexert themselves and thus cripple their muscles for the second day's work.

The second day should be devoted to teaching the men how to fall on the ball, along with an extra amount of running about, throwing and catching the ball.

The third day should find most of the candidates in proper condition to pursue their course of instruction in falling on the ball, and perhaps a few players might be singled out as desirable men to illustrate the principles of the way to boot the ball. Coaches should go light on having the men kick the ball at first, as very often a bad "Charlie Horse" is developed by too much kicking in the early days of practice.

The fourth day the candidates will be found to be sufficiently hardened up by their efforts in falling on the ball, and then teach them the proper way to approach and tackle the dummy. I might add here that ability to leave the feet and throw the body on either side in falling on the ball and in tackling the dummy should be taught the candidates. Very often a man will find it very much easier to leave the right foot than the left, while others will find the opposite the case, but a thorough drilling early in the season will, to a great extent, do away with this preference, and the sooner the better if an evenly developed squad of players is desired.

The fifth day should result in a thorough rehearsal of all of the above fundamentals, with individual instruction to the various players who have not perfected their work as well as many of the others. Ability to perform all of the fundamentals in a thoroughly competent manner is absolutely necessary before any of the other requirements of the game can be taken up. If all candidates show equal proficiency, they may be instructed in the proper manner of carrying the ball in the open as well as through the line of scrimmage. All candidates, whether they are to be used as line men or back-field players, should be taught the principles of carrying the ball.

The sixth day a few simple plays in offensive foot ball should be shown the candidates. Of course, this is after a division of the material is made, so that the fast, quick-thinking players have been assigned to the squad known as the back-field men, and the heavier ones have been assigned to another division known as line men. The end men may be taken from the line or back-field candidates, according to the judgment of the coach. A half-back very often proves a good end, while a fast, quick-witted tackle has proved to be equally effective.

When the simple plays have been mastered by the candidates, so that each and every man knows his place so perfectly that it will be next to an impossibility for him to mix up a play by not being in his right position, the individual coaching of the candidates relative to their respective duties at all times should be taken up.

The line should be taught to start with the ball, and the back-field likewise. On offense the line should be close together and the guards may lock legs with the center if they wish. Tackles play as close as possible to the guards and still afford ample protection to their back-field candidates. When the ends are on the line of scrimmage, but slightly outside of the opposing tackles, except when the opponents play so wide that they leave a large opening between their guard and tackle position, then the end should play close to his own tackle and call for a play through this opening. Backs should take a quick sprinter's start and manage to get their maximum speed up as soon as possible. On offense the three backs should be at least four yards in rear of the line of scrimmage and be separated by the distance of an arm's length. The quarter should be directly in back of his center and be the player to direct the attack by calling the signal.

A set of signals as simple as possible should be devised and furnished to each candidate for his study. A good course to follow in teaching signals and plays to candidates is for the coach to mark upon a blackboard the different plays, designating the position of each candidate at the start and completion of each play. More foot ball is taught by the use of the blackboard than by any other method that I know of. If a candidate can be made to understand the principles of every play, together with his respective duties in turning that play into a substantial gain, it is not probable that he will forget it as readily as he would if the coach only gave him his instruction on the field of play.

From simple play the team is gradually taught others of a more complex nature, until it has a repertoire of from ten to fifteen plays. It is a very good plan to enlarge this number as the season advances, but a great number of plays, where the candidates are only partly familiar with same, are far worse than too few. A great many of the large 'varsity teams number only twenty plays in their signals, while in a big game as few as six different formations have made up the entire offense of the winner's play.

A coach will do well if he will set aside the beginning of each day's practice to drill the candidates in a short rehearsal of the fundamentals of the game, as the team that perfects itself in these fundamental principles is the one that always proves to be the well greased, smooth running machine, as well as the championship combination. Also, the start of each day's practice should be devoted to having the squad of kickers boot the ball down the field to the back-field candidates to catch, and at the same time have the ends and line men go down under the kicks and tackle the man with the ball. In this way a squad of well conditioned, hard tackling players will be developed.

The ability of the backs to catch kicks and run them back successfully will also be developed considerably by this latter exercise. The proper way to take a man out in the open as well as to interfere for the man with the ball should be taught the men while at this open field work. This conforms to a great extent with the method used in tackling. The player should leave his feet, strike the opponent at a little above the knees with the shoulders, with the full weight of the body. Very often it will be found to be impossible to strike the opponent with the shoulder, as in the case of taking a man out from behind, then the back of the legs, close to the hips should be aimed at, so that if the distance is short, the body will cut him down by striking his legs. In making interference, a player is only held responsible for the blocking of one opponent. It is wrong in principle when it is planned to make him responsible for two or more opponents.

Ends, on the signal for a kick formation, should leave their places in the line, go out at least five or ten yards towards the side line and get a fast start with the ball. They should go straight down the field at as fast a rate of speed as possible and not look for the ball until they have heard the thud of the kicker's foot against it. Then they should turn, find the ball and close in sharply, keeping the kicker inside of them, and when sufficiently near, leave their feet and make a hard, clean tackle. The duty of an end at all times is to keep the man with the ball inside of him, because then others can bring the runner down, while outside he has a clear field.

The last and perhaps the most difficult department of foot ball for the novice to excel in is that of defense. The only correct way to teach defensive foot ball is to have a daily scrimmage between the first and second teams. If the fundamentals are properly developed, defensive foot ball will be the more easily taught.

Defense is divided into three departments, or rather, there are three lines of defense. Each line has three distinct duties to perform, on every play, and if each line carries out its work in a proper manner the offense of the opponents will go for naught.

The first line comprises the forwards of the team, center, guards, tackles and ends. They open up their line by spreading out across the field. The center plays up in the line opposite the opposing center, or else stands about a yard and a half or two yards back, as a "roving center." The guards leave their center and play opposite the hole between guard and tackle. The tackles about two yards from their guards, and just outside of the opposing tackles. The ends about three to six yards outside of their tackles.

Three distinct duties devolve upon each of the forwards. First, they charge into their opponent's territory by using their hands or shoulders; second, they find the play; and third, they either get their bodies across the play, or else, where they have a clear try at the man with the ball, they make the tackle. Waiting ends vary slightly, inasmuch as they make their first move by charging in at right angles to the line of scrimmage for at least two yards; second, they turn in to meet the play, and third, they either turn the play inside of them or make the tackle. A smashing end will play the game as described in the first instance.

The second line of defense consists of the three backs. The halves, who safeguard the flanks in the open style game, are required to play approximately six or eight yards in the rear, and at least three yards outside of their tackles, thereby making the defense for all open play more practical. The back, who makes all plays directed at the center of the line safe, plays about four or five yards in the rear of his center.

The duties of this second line are also three in number. First, not to move until they know exactly where the ball has gone; this is to keep them from being tricked by a delayed or double pass; second, after finding the ball they get to it with all possible speed; and third, they make the tackle, whether it is an end run or a play through the line. On kick formations the ends drop back a couple of yards in rear of their own scrimmage lines, making all fake kicks safe, while the two flank half-backs follow the opposing ends out and block them from going down the field and making the tackle. The center defensive back, who is generally the full-back because of his added weight over the quarter, goes back to assist the man who is laying back to make the catch. Each takes a side of the field and thereby decreases the possibility of the opposing kicker booting the ball to an unoccupied spot.

The third line of defense consists of the quarter-back, who plays twenty-five or thirty yards in rear of his line of scrimmage. Never should this man come closer to his forwards than twenty-five yards, or else a quick kick by the opponents will result in the ball being booted over his head with disastrous results. Nor should this player come up on the run to meet a play, as it is less difficult for the man with the ball to dodge him if he is running towards him, than if he waits, sets himself and meets him with a hard, sure tackle.

As a final suggestion to prep school coaches, I would advise them not to allow their charges to engage in a contest where the opponents outweigh them greatly or where they are more mature. It is all right to win over a bigger and stronger rival, but very often the cost of serious injury offsets this extra amount of glory. Most accidents in foot ball result from attempts on the part of younger, lighter and more inexperienced players to conquer big, massive rivals. Also, short quarters should be indulged in early in the season, and only in final championship games should the regulation quarters of fifteen minutes be allowed.

Training for Foot Ball

BY THE LATE MICHAEL MURPHY,

For Many Years Director of Athletics at the University of Pennsylvania.

The days of the extremes of training, both in foot ball and other sports, have, at any rate for the time being, gone by. The old-fashioned notion that men must be deprived of everything they wanted for their comfort and go through a period of actual physical suffering has been exploded. Young men, and particularly college men, do not need the severe regimen adopted in the old days, when training was confined only to a certain class and that class one indulging in all sorts of dissipation between times. For this reason treatises on training can be far more brief than in the times when the exact percentage of food stuffs was figured out to a nicety. Moreover, foot ball is one of those fortunate sports which comes at a season of the year when the weather, except in the very early part of it, is not exceedingly hot, but rather bracing, and unless there is something radically wrong with the man, as a rule, during the foot ball season, his appetite should in the main improve.

It is really the nervous tension which has come to be great and it is to the relief of that nervous tension that many of the best friends of the game are looking in hopes that alterations in the rules may improve this condition.

The great majority of the players are not affected by this, but the captain, coach and quarter-back usually pass through periods where the worry is quite extreme, and while it makes little difference to the coach, it does affect the captain and quarter-back very materially, and with these men, the greatest problem of the training season is to see that they pay less rather than more attention to the sport and get some relaxation at periods.

The general physical condition of the men is in these days looked after both by the trainer and by competent surgeons, so far as injuries are concerned.

The problem of how much work a man should do and when he should work is one of general consultation between coach, trainer and captain—the trainer's opinion being in the main accepted as final—and as a rule this trio make satisfactory decisions. Sometimes a man is found who is able to deceive all three as to his condition, but not often, and, moreover, such men are usually men whose personal idiosyncrasies are known.

One of the most difficult points in training a foot ball team is to keep them steadily progressing and not have a slump at some disastrous period during the season. Men differ so greatly individually that the accepted method of working the men nowadays is to watch these peculiarities and not try to judge all men by the same rule, but to lay off first one and then another as occasion demands, giving them all an opportunity for sufficient practice, but forcing no man to work too long.

It takes a good deal of time to teach a man modern foot ball and he has to go through a certain period of steady work before he combines the necessary knowledge with the skill; hence an especial reason for consistency in carrying out training development. Foot ball men all need quickness and the work should be devoted to short periods of snappy play rather than long periods which get the man into the bad habit of playing slowly because he is tired.

A foot ball player beyond all else needs to have a sort of superfluous energy to draw upon at the time of his match, and to exhaust this is to make a very serious mistake. The men should, therefore, be very carefully watched in order to see that the work is not at the expense of this energy, which must be called upon at a critical time. No man should find himself in a game without a feeling that he would at least like to make a touchdown whether it is possible or not, and the making of touchdowns is practically impossible if the man's physical and mental condition is such as to leave him without desire to do so.

The first problem in the season that faces captain, coaches and trainers is that of making selection from a great mass of material. This material will be scattered over three or four different fields and in all sorts of physical condition, as some men take care of themselves during the summer, while others do not. A coach may easily be deceived by lack of condition in a man who, when in shape, would play a strong game. For this reason critical watching and very likely some inquiry as to the past performance of the man is very advisable. As soon as the material has begun to be sifted it becomes necessary to sort out a part of it for the 'varsity, but it is wise not to take a great many men to a training table early but make this rather a reward of merit in a way, at the same time taking possibly the absolutely sure men who are not likely to have the best of living otherwise.

All this matter is a question of judgment and a little study and reflection on the subject is returned many times over in the results later in the season. It is hardly worth while, although I know it has been adopted by some trainers, to put men who are going to play foot ball through special courses of gymnastics, unless it may be for some special weakness of the individual. It is certainly a good plan for foot ball men to be handled by a track trainer in learning to start quickly. Gymnasium apparatus, however, is not proving very successful for general teams. A little setting up work in the early part of the season is often a good thing and some running, but after the season is once under way the men have plenty to do without taking these special exercises, except it may be to reduce the weight of a man who is very heavy. Running around the field for men who are temporarily laid off, and for the whole squad in the early part of the season, is a good thing.

Another great problem is to keep enough backs and, since the introduction of the new rules, ends as well, to last through the season. The backs are usually lighter than the forwards and being given a good deal more of the running work to do (and this is particularly true under the new rules where the men behind the line will have to do a good deal of line hammering without heavy interference) is rather apt to call for all the material that a coach and trainer can keep going. And even then at the end of the season the good men are scarce. The first part of the season the practice ought to be very short—four or five minutes—and the team work up to longer periods as the weather grows cooler and they improve in condition. By mid-season they should be able to play two fifteen-minute halves with ease, and if possible a fifteen and twenty-minute half. By November they should be able to stand a slightly longer period in order that by the time of the big games they may be able to go the necessary two thirty-five minute halves.

As to protectors for the players, it is well worth while to use such protectors as are likely to save the players from injury, but of late it is feared too much has been done in this way so that the players were rendered rather less plucky, and, moreover, in some instances were probably made tender. Under the present rules the doing away with the heavy head protectors will be a great step in advance and will probably save many injuries. Nose guards are rather difficult to breathe through, but properly arranged are not dangerous. Protectors for the thigh and shins are good things and if a man receives an injured shoulder some kind of protection there is also advisable.

So far as foot ball is concerned a strict diet is not essential, but the men should not be permitted to smoke, nor should they be given alcoholic drinks except for medicinal purposes or when a man is very tired. The living should be plain and substantial and every effort made to have his training table attractive and the food appetizing.

Early Fall Practice

All the large teams nowadays are in the habit of doing some practice in the fall preparatory to the work in the line-up. This kind of practice, if properly organized, is of considerable benefit, but when it is merely disjointed and carelessly arranged it does little if any good to any one except the kickers. The same kind of work should be done in the spring, hence a description of fall practice should cover any kind of practice performed with the team when scrimmaging is inadvisable.

When the men turn out in the fall the squad usually includes several men who perhaps have not played on the team before, and some very likely who have never been out trying for it. It is, therefore, advisable for the captain to have three or four of his coaches on hand and, on the first day, or even preparatory to that first day, secure the names and addresses, also age and weight and probable position of each candidate. Then he starts off with a knowledge of what men he has, their relative weights and the position each man thinks himself best qualified for. It may prove, and very likely will, that he may shift the men from the positions they intended trying for to others, but he should start off with the probability that the men themselves know approximately what their capabilities are.

On the first day he should run his squad once or twice around the field for a breather and then break them up into organizations as follows: He should take his centers, quarters, and backs and separate them from his line men, with the exception of the ends. He should then place, say at one end of the field, all his line men, and if he has enough to make two groups of six, so much the better. As many groups of six as he has of line men should be separated and put under the charge of a coach. Their work should then consist of charging on the snap of the ball, the coach giving the signals by standing with his hand on the ball and giving it a turn. He should then practice them all on falling on the ball, rolling the ball along and calling out the man who is to fall on it or taking turns at this. This should be done with each squad of line men and with considerable moderation the first day, gradually working up to longer work. Then it is well to run each of these squads, say a quick run on the snap of the ball of twenty yards. Meantime, the other squad, consisting of centers, quarters and backs, grouped at the other end of the field, should be broken up into groups of fives, consisting of a center, quarter, two halves and a back. These men should be given a set of simple signals, covering a run around the end, straight line buck, cross-buck and kick. The center puts the ball in play after the quarter has called the signal and the men run through the play, moving the ball about four or five yards to the play, and thus proceeding for half the length of the field and then turn around and come back. On the kick it is not necessary to kick the ball, but the center should toss it to the full-back as he stands back in position for a kick. It is well to shift so that the back-field men get a chance with different quarters and also so that the quarters get practice with different centers.

The ends should be formed in a separate group by themselves and they should practice in the following manner:

Divide them into sets of four and separate them in pairs about half the breadth of the field across the field. Then let them start running down the field, passing the ball across from one pair to another, letting them take turns in catching and passing.

It will be found that this work is rather fatiguing and long before the line men and the groups of centers and quarters have become exhausted in their work, the ends will have had plenty of running exercise. Then the ends should come in and change places with the half-backs, while the half-backs, in groups of four, run down the field, throwing the ball the same as have the ends. Then certain of the ends should go in and take the position of quarters, to get practice in handling the ball, while a portion of the half-backs and backs go out and practice kicking and catching long punts.

In this practice it is well to have two centers detailed to go out and pass the ball back for the kick.

When the men have become somewhat hardened up, it is wise to have the tackles perform the same work as before outlined for the ends, that they too may become accustomed to catching and throwing the ball. Furthermore, if the track trainer is available it would be excellent to have him take hold of the big line men a little at this season of the year and teach them to start quickly. Always bear in mind the fact that they should start principally from a crouching position, being well over their feet, and shooting forward and up at the same time.

[It is customary in spring practice to have prizes for kicking, both drop-kicking and punts, for distance and accuracy. It is also a good plan to have prizes for distance and accuracy of forward passing. It is not a bad thing to add to this, as a finale, two foot races, the contestants each to carry a ball. If this is attempted, the backs, ends and quarters should form one group, and here it will be necessary to run the race off in heats, the distance being fifty-five yards, while the tackles should form another group, the distance for these being forty-five yards; the guards and centers a third group, the distance for them being thirty yards. Bear in mind that each man should carry a ball, and if he drops the ball he is disqualified.]

Considerable care should be taken in the early part of the fall practice, as well as in the early part of the spring practice, not to overwork the men in the first day or two, particularly if they are not in the best of condition. The time for the first day should be short and not energetic, but after a few days every part of the practice, even though short, should be snappy, and accuracy should be insisted upon. If a squad, for instance, of center, quarter and backs are fumbling the ball they should be reprimanded and be sent through a dozen plays, with instructions not to fumble a single ball, to even go slower, if necessary, and then after performing properly a dozen times they should be speeded up again. Great insistence should also be placed upon accuracy of the punters and no carelessness or looseness in catching these punts. Every punt should be caught and not carelessly fumbled, for whatever habits are instilled then will probably hold later on.

There are certain times later in the season when a little morning practice is very advisable for individual men on the team, especially those developing faults or needing some correction. This is apt to be particularly true of centers in their passing and quarter-backs in handling the ball. Fortunately this is the easiest kind of a combination to work, because the two men can get together on any spot near their rooms and work out for half an hour or so in the morning. It is necessary also to see that they do not practice too long or get too tired of the monotony, as they will perhaps if they have this morning practice and play full halves in the afternoon.

If room can be obtained it is well to give the backs practice in kicking and catching at certain times during the season in the morning. This is especially necessary in place-kicking goals, drop-kicking and practising forward passes. Where the field is far removed from the university or school, facilities for morning practice can usually be obtained nearer at hand, although with some inconvenience.

Signals

BY TOM THORP AND ED THORP.

Simplicity should be the keynote of every system of foot ball signals. The less intricate and complex the system, the more efficient they are bound to prove. Nothing militates so much against successful team play as does a complicated system of signals. Such a set not only troubles a quarter-back in framing his signals, but confuses the minds of the individual players to such an extent that it deprives the team of that confidence of play that is so vital to success.

With a plain, simple set of signals, the quarter is enabled to rattle them off as he would his a, b, c's and the players grasp their meaning immediately, with the result that the execution of play would be fast and snappy. In no other way can a team be developed into a well balanced machine than by the installation of a simple set of signals.

It does not follow because your signals are simple that the opponents will be able to solve them. The chances are very much against any such state of affairs. In fact, a team that takes its attention off the play to interpret the signals of an opponent would find themselves at such a disadvantage that it would not be long before they would find their own goal line in jeopardy. Never in the history of foot ball has a team been able to vanquish an opponent by solving their system of signals. On the other hand, many teams have defeat chalked up against them because of this foolish practice. The loss of the "jump on the ball" is too great a disadvantage to overcome in any way.

Occasionally a team becomes wise to the signals, especially if the same play is attempted several times in succession. To safeguard against this, in every set of signals given in this article provision is made for a change which is in keeping with the simplicity of the code.

In arranging any set of signals there are always two things to be taken into consideration—the quarter-back or player who calls the signals, and the remainder of the team. The signals should be such as will enable the quarter-back to rattle them off fast and accurately. The quarter-back who hesitates should be sent to the side lines for further tutelage. He should be so familiar with his signals that he can rattle any of them off without the least hesitation and be able to use the correct one when he needs it. Not only is this the first duty of a quarter-back, but the rest of the team should be as familiar with the code as that player himself. Too much time and attention cannot be given to drilling a team in its signals, as the speed and offensive strength of an eleven is traceable to their intimacy with their code of signals.

Often a quarter-back will call his signals and then turn around and look to see if all the other members of the team have grasped the signals. This is fatal. There should be no wait. As soon as a signal has been called the ball should be put in play and the play denoted by the signal executed. It is the speed with which a quarter-back calls his signals, and the promptness of the team to execute them, upon which depends the ultimate success of each play. The two systems of signals given in this article have been built upon those fundamental principles. They have both been tried and found to conform to the demands of all situations.

In diagrams the black, solid square denotes the player taking the ball; the heavy continuous line the direction the players take after the ball has been snapped; the zig-zag line shows how the ball reaches him; the dash and dot line indicates direction of forward pass; and the dotted squares indicate changes in position assumed by the players in such a play as a "shift," etc.

To indicate the positions the following abbreviations have been adopted: L.E., left end; L.T., left tackle; L.G., left guard; C., center; R.G., right guard; R.T., right tackle; R.E., right end; Q.B., quarter-back; L.H., left half-back; R.H., right half-back; F.B., full-back. Where O is used, it will indicate that the player is occupying a position on the defensive.

The most practical system of signals, and one that is used by a number of the large college teams, is the one of numbering the plays. A number of examples of such is as follows;

2. L.H. around R.E.
3. R.H. around L.E.
4. R.H. through R.T.
5. L.H. through L.T.
6. F.B. through R.G.
7. F.B. through L.G.
8. L.H. cross on R.T.
9. R.H. cross on L.T.
10. Q.B. around R.E.
12. L.E. around R.E.
13. R.E. around L.E.
14. L.T. around R.T.
15. R.T. around L.T.
16. F.B. on delayed pass through R.G.
17. F.B. on delayed pass through L.G.
18. L.H. on delayed pass through R.T.
19. R.H. on delayed pass through L.T.
20. Q.B. around L.E.
22. Forward pass to R.E.
23. Forward pass to L.E.
24. Forward pass to R.H. or Q.B.
25. Forward pass to L.H. or Q.B.
26. Forward pass to R.T.
27. Forward pass to L.T.
28. Double pass, L.H. to R.H.
29. Double pass, R.H. to L.H.
30. Q.B. on direct pass through C.
32. F.B. fake kick around R.E.
33. F.B. fake kick around L.E.
34. L.H. fake forward pass around R.E.
36. Q.B. fake place-kick around R.E.
37. Q.B. fake place-kick around L.E.
38. Q.B. fake kick through R.G.

Signal for regular punts will be any number ending in one, below 50, as 11, 21, 31, 41. For a drop-kick or place-kick the same numbers are used, but before calling signals, quarter-back will call drop-kick or place-kick formation.

On shift formation, where a direct pass is made to the player who is to carry the ball, the signal shall be the same as if the ball had been first passed to the quarter-back and in turn passed to the back-field man.

For the on-side kick, which is generally made from a regular formation, by a direct pass to the man making the kick, the signal may be any number above 50, or a series in which all of the last digits of the numbers used are 0, as 50, 60, 70.

The way the above signals should be given is as follows: The signal number may be made the second number of the series and the series contain three different numbers, as 9, 2, 6. The signal number being the second number of the series, the signal would read L.H. around R.E.; again, as 5, 4, 7—L.H. through L.T.; again, 54, 23, 3—forward pass to L.E., and so on.

If a change was made and the signal number was changed to read the third number of the series, then 4, 9, 7—F.B. through L.G. and 15, 30, 24—forward pass to R.H., and so on.

If another change was thought advisable and the signal number was made to read the first number, then 4, 5, 2—R.H. through R.T. and 25, 34, 56—forward pass to L.H., and so on.

It is thought advisable for the quarter-back to repeat the series. This is more of a precautionary measure than anything else, but it is a very good plan to follow, as, 2, 3, 9—2, 3, 9 and 7, 4, 6—7, 4, 6. In this way the men are given a sufficient time to fathom the signal, and it will time the play much better than if you only called the series once and have the ball passed at the completion of it. Then, again, some players take a longer time to fathom a signal than others, and the same smoothness of play would not result from calling the series once, as if the series was repeated. Therefore, to have complete smoothness and the correct interval between plays, the repeating of the series is the best policy to follow.

In the series used with diagrams, second number of the series is the signal number.

Then we have the system in which both players and holes are numbered. Starting with L.E. 1, L.T. 3, L.G. 5, R.G. 6, R.T. 4, R.E. 2, L.H. 7, R.H. 8, F.B. 9, and Q.B. 0. Hole outside L.E., 1, between L.E. and L.T. 3, L.T. and L.G. 5, L.G. and C. 7, C. and R.G. 8, R.G. and R.T. 6, R.T. and R.E. 4, and outside R.E. 2. The last digit of the first number is through which hole the play is going, and the last digit of the second number signifies who is to carry the ball, as 25, 37, 42, the last number being a fake, would be L.H. through the hole between L.T. and L.G.; again, 23, 54, 39 would be R.T. through the hole between L.E. and L.T. This system has been used with success at many of the leading prep schools.

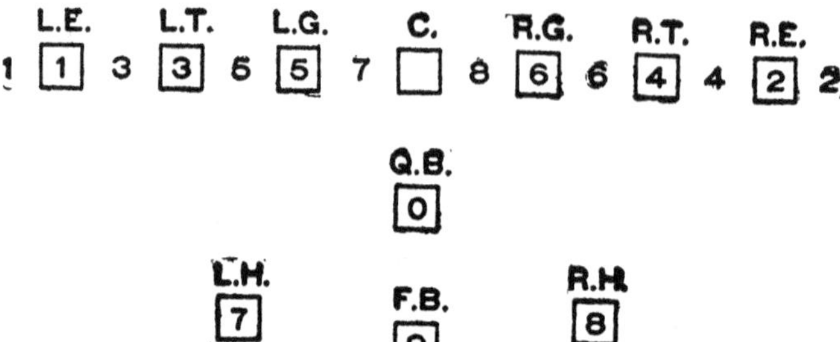

In the plays that follow we use the first system of signals, the second number being the play.

Signal 5, as 8, 5, 9.
Straight buck on left side, with L.H. carrying ball.

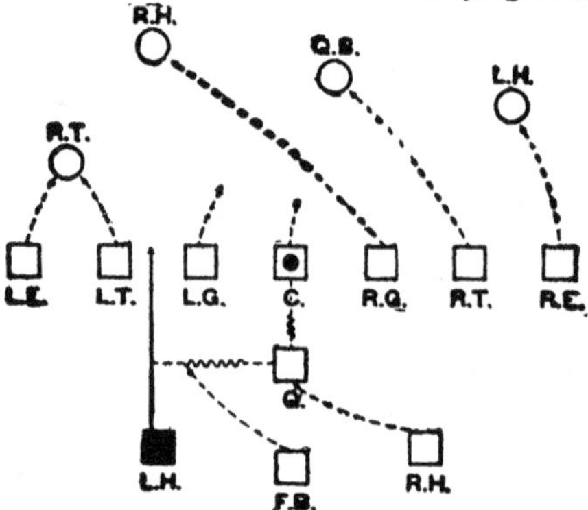

L.E. and L.T. block R.T.; L.G. and C. block their opponents; R.G., R.T. and R.E. take off secondary defense; Q.B. receives ball from C. and makes quick pass to L.H.; F.B. and R.H. follow through, making the play safe.

Signal 4, as 6, 4, 3.
Straight buck on right side, with R.H. carrying ball.

L.H.
Q.B.
R.H.
L.T.
L.E.
L.T.
L.G.
C.
R.G.
R.T.
R.E.
Q.
L.H.
F.B.
R.H.

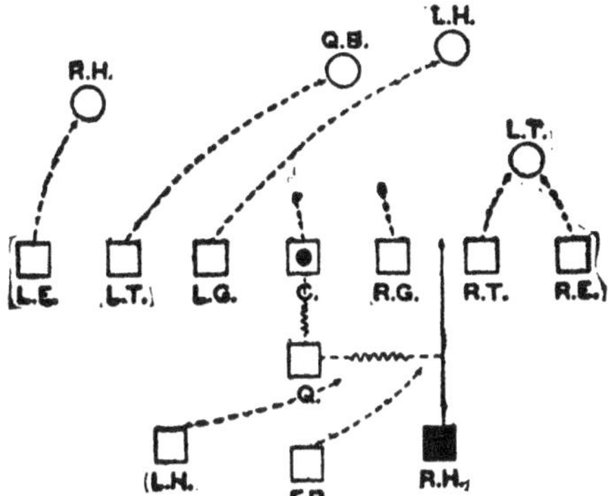

R.E. and R.T. block L.T.; R.G. and C. block their opponents; L.G., L.T. and L.E. pick off secondary defense; Q.B. receives ball from C. and makes a quick pass to R.H.; F.B. and L.H. follow through, making the play safe.

Very often the F.B. is sent ahead of the man with the ball.

Signal 7, as 4, 7, 5.
Full-back straight through L.G.

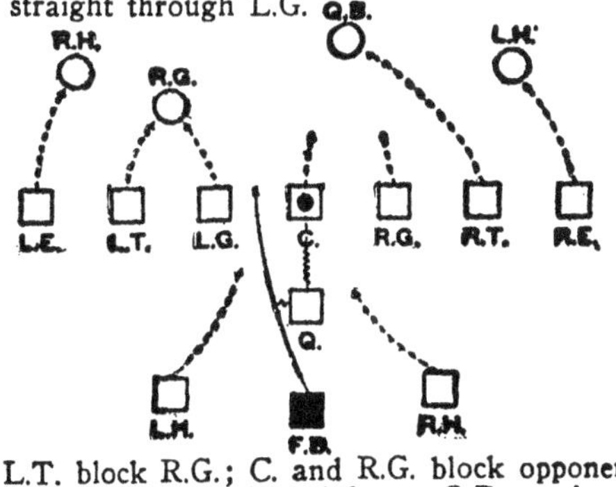

Q.B.
R.H.
L.H.
R.G.
L.E.
L.T.
L.G.
C.
R.G.
R.T.
R.E.
Q.
L.H.
F.B.
R.H.

L.G. and L.T. block R.G.; C. and R.G. block opponents; L.E., R.T. and R.E. pick off secondary defense; Q.B. receives ball and makes quick pass to FB.; L.H. and R.H. follow through, making play safe. Very often the L.H. is sent ahead of the F.B.

Signal 6, as 9, 6, 5.
Full-back straight through the R.G.

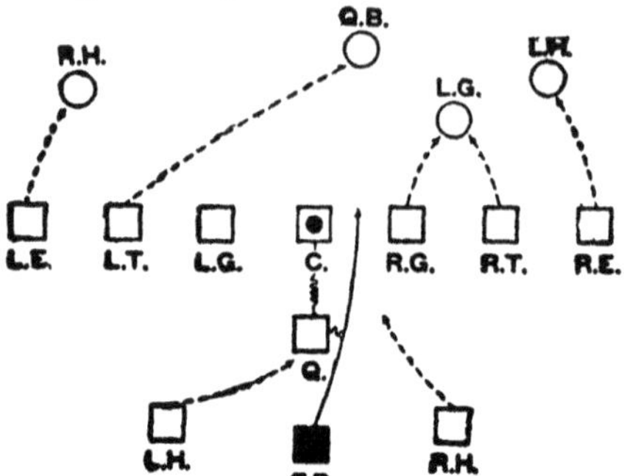

R.G. and R.T. block L.G.; C. and L.G. block their opponents; R.E., L.T. and L.E. pick off the secondary defense; Q.B. receives the ball from C. and makes a quick pass to F.B.; R.H. and L.H. follow through, making the play safe.

Very often the R.H. is sent ahead of the man with the ball.

Signal 8, as 5, 8, 3.
Cross-buck with L.H. carrying ball over R.T.

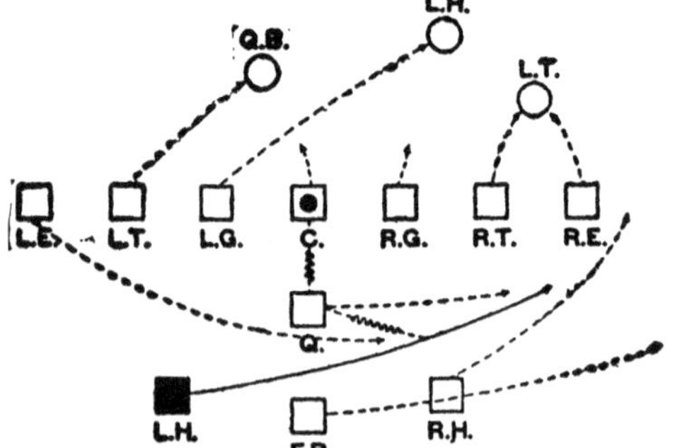

R.E. and R.T. block L.T.; R.G. and C. block their opponents; L.G. and L.T. pick off secondary defense; L.E. follows in rear of play, making it safe; Q.B. receives ball from C. and passes it to L.H.; R.H. goes ahead of ball and cleans up outside of tackle; F.B. takes care of defensive end.

Signal 9, as 6, 9, 5.
Cross-buck with the R.H. carrying the ball over L.T.

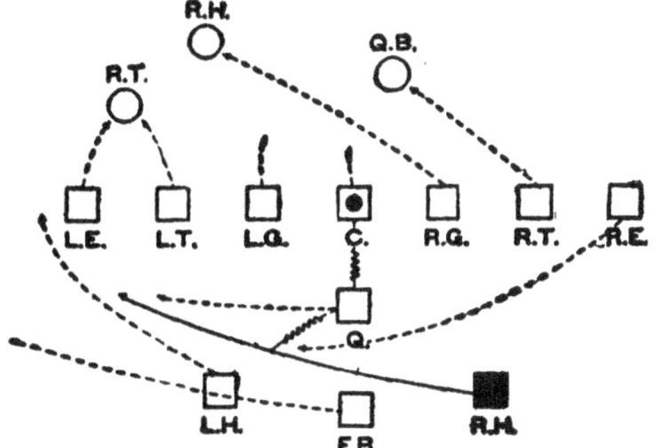

L.E. and L.T. block R.T.; L.G. and C. block opponents; R.G. and R.T. pick off secondary defense; Q.B. receives ball from C. and makes pass to R.H.; L.H. goes ahead of ball and cleans up; F.B. takes care of defensive end and R.E. follows play around from rear, making it safe.

Signal 2, as 5, 2, 4.
Run around R.E., with L.H. carrying the ball.

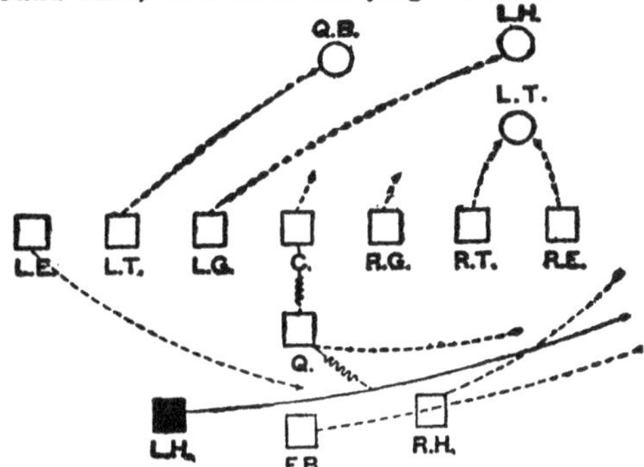

R.E. and R.T. block L.T.; R.G. and C. block opponents; L.G. and L.T. pick off secondary defense; Q.B. receives ball from C. and passes to L.H.; R.H. leads interference; F.B. takes care of defensive end, and L.E. follows around in rear, making play safe.

Signal 3, as 8, 3, 7.
Run around L.E., with R.H. carrying the ball.

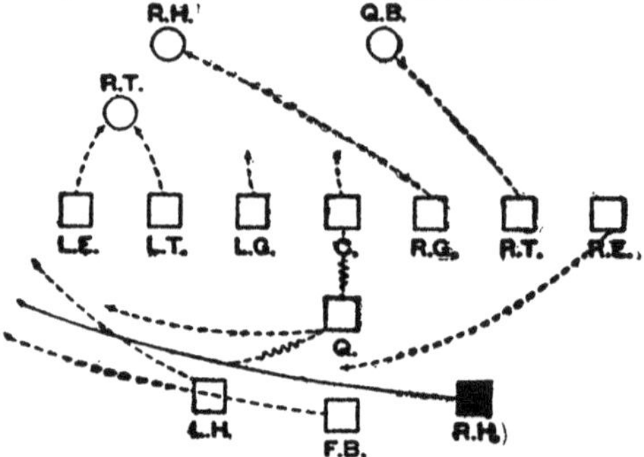

L.E. and L.T. block R.T.; L.G. and C. block opponents; R.G. and R.T. pick off secondary defense; Q.B. receives ball from C. and passes to R.H.; L.H. leads interference; F.B. takes care of defensive end and R.E. follows play from the rear, making it safe.

Signal 10, as 15, 10, 4.
Quarter-back carrying ball around R.E.

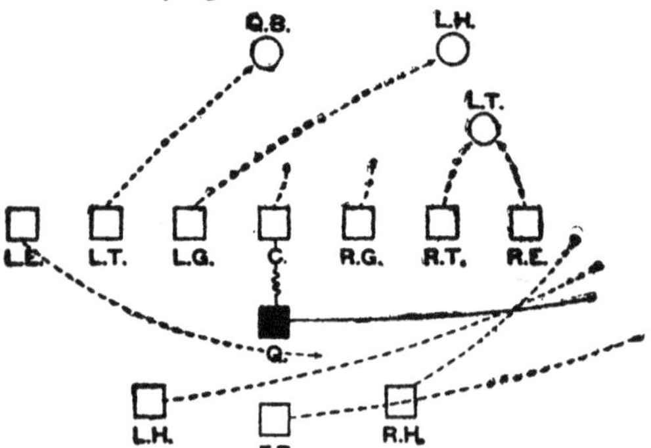

R.E. and R.T. block L.T.; R.G. and C. block opponents, L.G. and L.T. pick off secondary defense; R.H. leads interference; L.H. joins interference; Q.B. receives ball from C. and runs wide; F.B. takes care of defensive end, and L.E. follows in rear of play and makes it safe.

Signal 20, as 8, 20, 16.
Quarter-back carrying ball around L.E.

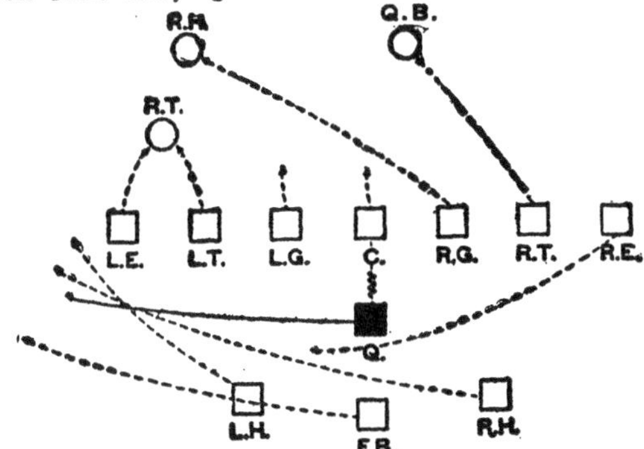

L.E. and L.T. block R.T.; L.G. and C. block opponents; R.G. and R.T. pick off secondary defense; L.H. leads interference; R.H. joins interference; F.B. takes care of defensive end; Q.B. receives ball and runs wide; R.E. follows play in rear and makes it safe.

Signal 15, as 8, 15, 19.
R.T. carrying ball through L.T.

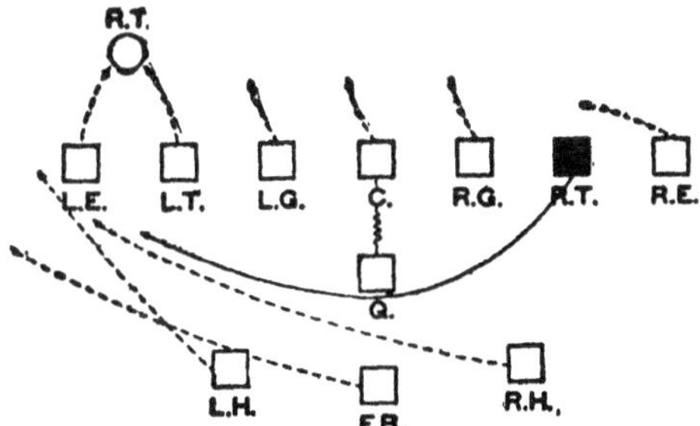

L.E. and L.T. block R.T.; L.G., C. and R.G. block opponents and then go through for secondary defense; R.E. charges into hole left by R.T.; R.T. pivots on inside foot and runs over L.T.; Q.B. receives ball from C. and passes it to R.T. as he goes by; L.H. and R.H. "clean up;" F.B. goes out for defensive end.

Signal 14, as 11, 14, 5.
L.T. carrying ball through R.T.

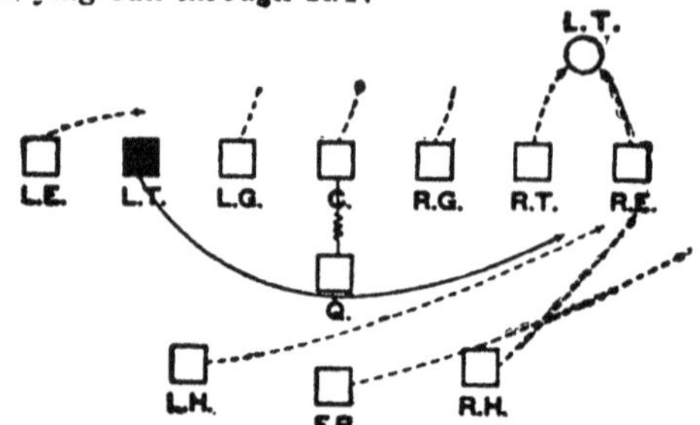

R.E. and R.T. block L.T.; R.G., C. and L.G. block opponents and then go through for secondary defense; L.E. charges into hole left by L.T.; L.T. pivots on inside foot and runs over R.T.; Q.B. receives ball from C. and passes it to L.T. as he goes by; R.H. and L.H. "clean up;" F.B. goes out for defensive end.

Signal: Kick formation, 41, as 35, 41, 24.
Punt from kick formation.

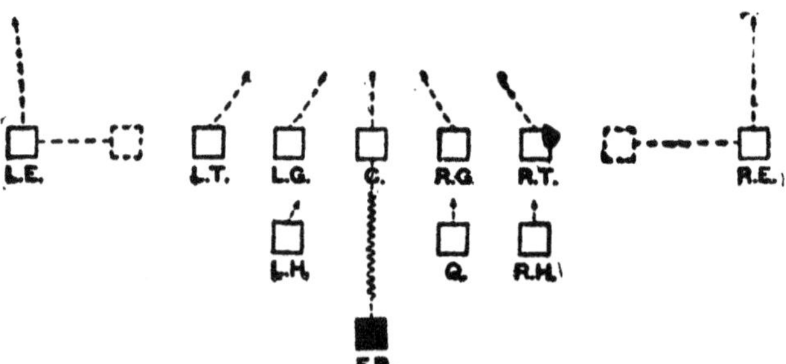

R.G. and L.G lock legs with C.; R.T. and L.T. make everything inside safe; R.E. and L.E. go out at least 4 or 5 yards; L.H. moves up in rear of L.G. and about 3 yards back; Q.B. 3 yards in rear of R.G.; R.H. 3 yards in rear of R.T.; F.B. 10 yards in rear of C. when ball is snapped; R.E. and L.E. go straight down field. Line men hold momentarily and then go down under kick; L.H., Q.B. and R.H. pick off opponents who charge past line men; F.B. kicks the ball.

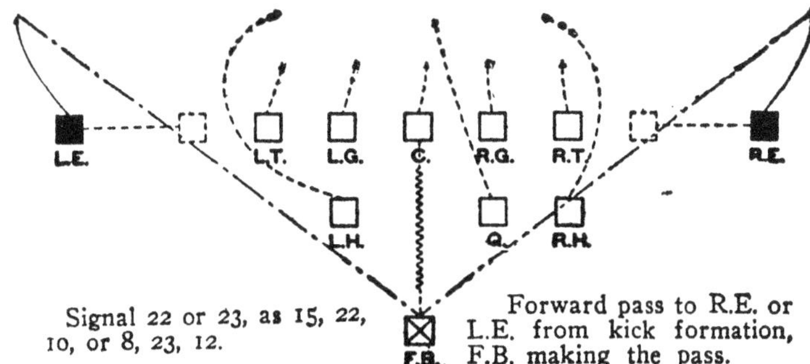

Signal 22 or 23, as 15, 22, 10, or 8, 23, 12.

Forward pass to R.E. or L.E. from kick formation, F.B. making the pass.

The players assume the positions as in a kick formation; when ball is snapped, R.E. and L.E. run wide and attempt to elude their opponents; L.H. and R.H. run outside of tackle position and place themselves in rear of opponents' line of scrimmage; Q.B. sifts through scrimmage line and calls for ball; line men hold opponents from charging through and spoiling pass; F.B. receives ball from center and glances to see if R.E. or L.E. are uncovered; finding either one so, he passes the ball to him.

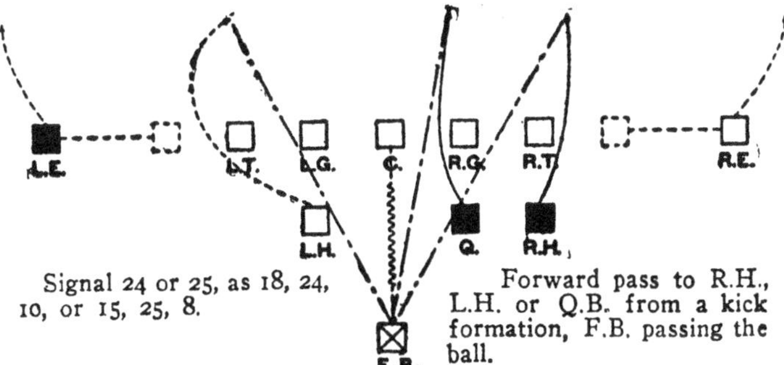

Signal 24 or 25, as 18, 24, 10, or 15, 25, 8.

Forward pass to R.H., L.H. or Q.B. from a kick formation, F.B. passing the ball.

The players assume the positions as in a kick formation; when the ball is snapped, R.E. and L.E. run out wide and shout for ball; L.H., R.H. and Q.B. cut around in back of opponents; line men hold fast, not allowing anyone to sift through them; the ball is snapped to F.B.; he glances at the three back men, finds one uncovered and makes the pass to him.

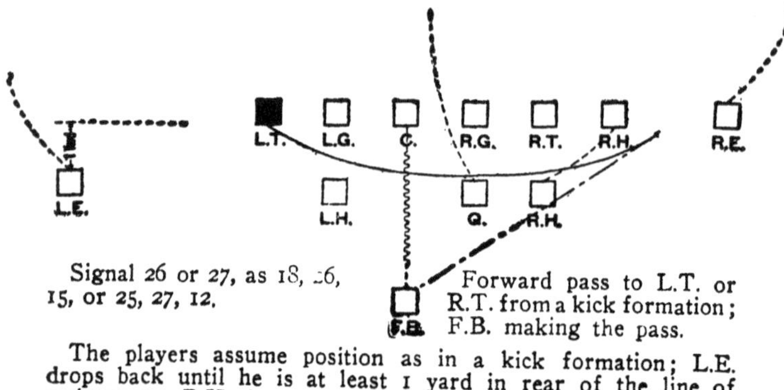

Signal 26 or 27, as 18, 26, 15, or 25, 27, 12.

Forward pass to L.T. or R.T. from a kick formation; F.B. making the pass.

The players assume position as in a kick formation; L.E. drops back until he is at least 1 yard in rear of the line of scrimmage; R.H. jumps up on scrimmage line, making seven men there, with L.T. occupying the left hand extremity, thus being eligible to receive forward pass; R.E. and L.E. run out wide and shout for ball; L.H. charges into anyone who may follow L.T.; Q.B. sifts through line; L.T. runs in rear of his line; F.B. receives ball from C. and as L.T. crosses line of scrimmage makes the pass to him. The same play may be used on the opposite side of the line, with R.T. receiving ball by having the R.E. drop back one yard and the L.H. on line of scrimmage. If tackle is not free to receive pass, a long pass can be made to either end.

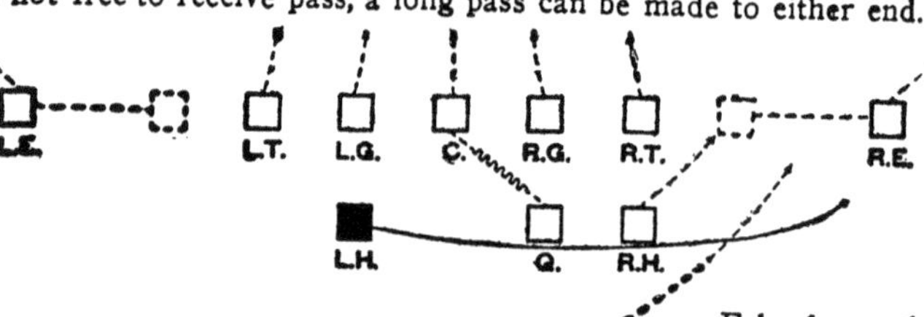

Signal 34, as 18, 34, 10.

Fake forward pass from kick formation with L.H. carrying the ball around R.E.

The players assume position as in kick formation; ball passed to Q.B., who fakes a forward pass; L.H. shoots around in rear of Q.B. and takes ball off his hand as it is drawn back for a pass; R.H. and F.B. form an interference. The play should be a wide, sweeping one.

Signal 32 or 33, as 12, 32, 50, or 15, 33, 8.
Fake kick, with F.B. carrying ball around R.E. or L.E.

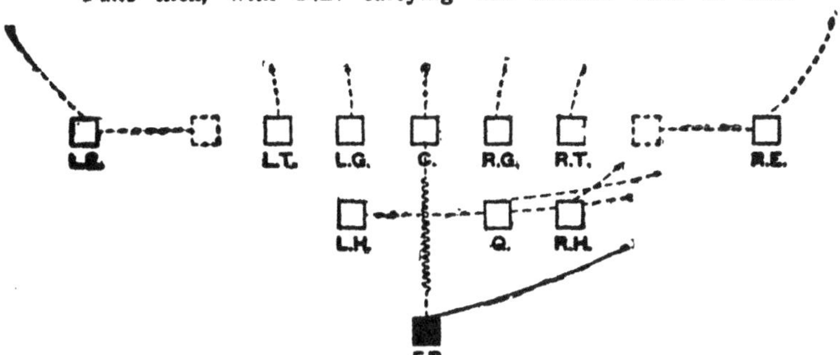

The players assume position, as in a kick formation; the ball is passed to F.B. and he starts on a wide sweep around R.E., R.H. Q.B. and L.H. forming his interference; the same play may be made around L.E.

Signal 38, as 20, 38, 12.
Fake kick, with Q.B. carrying ball through R.G.

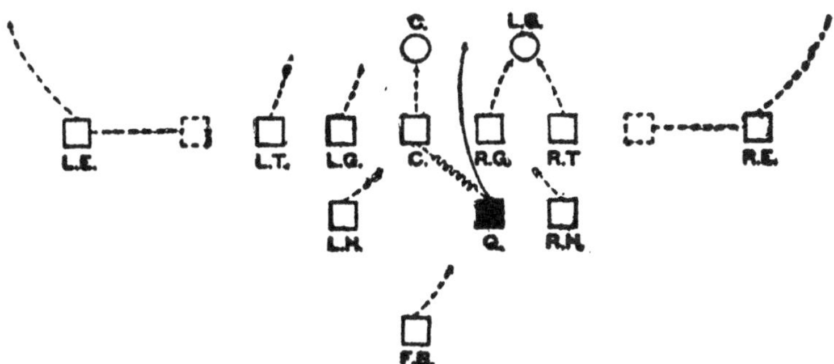

The players assume positions, as in kick formation; the R.G. and R.T. block the L.G.; C. blocks his opponent; Q.B. receives the ball and makes a quick break through R.G.

Signal 3, as 8, 3, 7.

Shift formation with a direct pass to R.H. for run around L.E. The players assume position as in regular formation. The signal is called after the word "shift." Immediately the players shift to Position II.

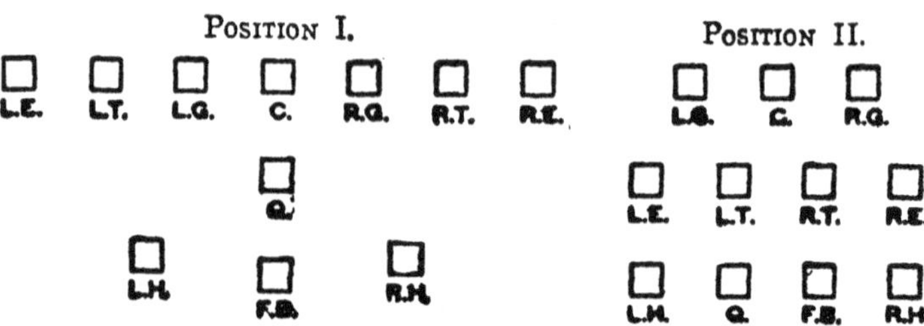

Then word "shift" is repeated. The players shift to following position, and as soon as they come to a standstill the ball is passed and the play is off.

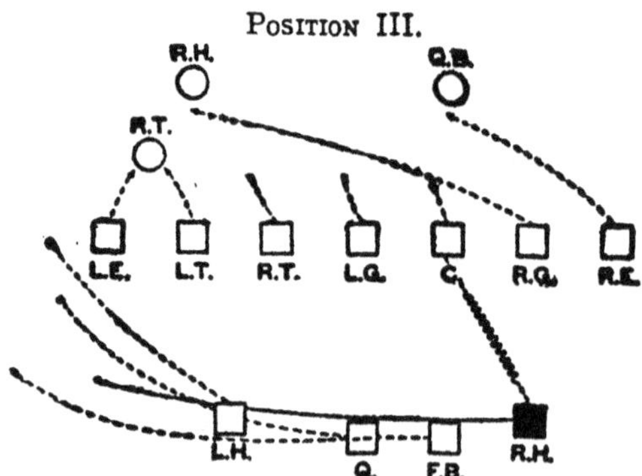

L.E. and L.T. block R.T.; L.T., R.T., L.G. and C. block opponents; R.G. and R.E. pick off secondary defense; L.H. leads interference; Q.B. takes defensive end; F.B. joins interference and the ball is snapped to R.H. and he runs wide.

The same play may be made with L.H. carrying ball around R.E.; the shift is to the right instead of left, as in diagram.

Signal 12 or 13, as 14, 12, 8, or 9, 13, 17.
A formation to right with L.E. carrying ball around R.E. or R.E. around L.E.

POSITION I.

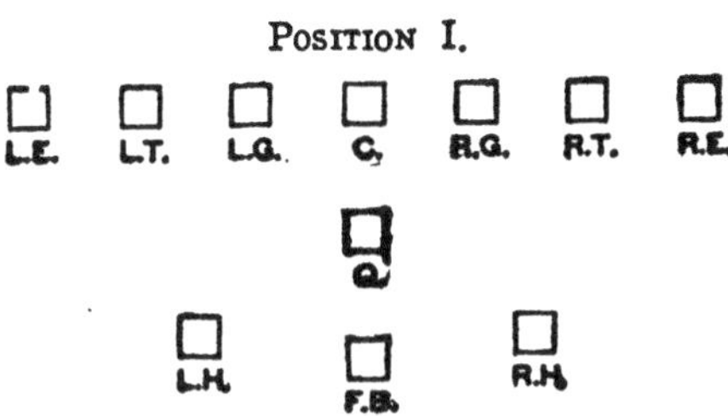

"Formation right" is called, then

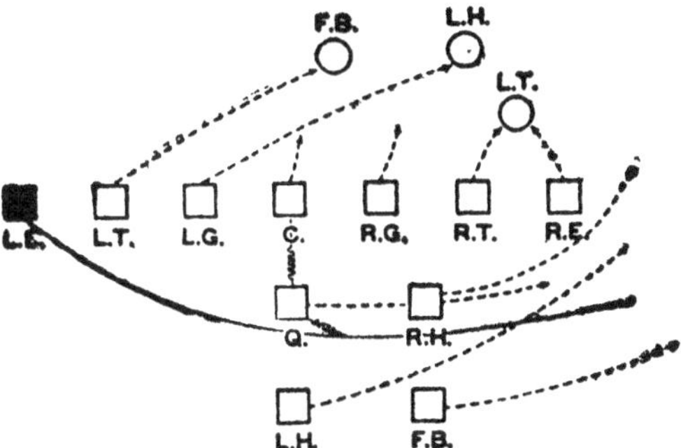

R.E. and R.T. block L.T.; R.G. and C. block opponents; L.G. and L.T. take secondary defense; R.H. and L.H. make interference; F.B. takes defensive end; Q.B. receives ball from C. and passes it to L.E. as he passes him; L.E. must be a very fast man to make the play effective. The same play may be used with R.E. carrying ball around L.E.

Signal 17 or 16, as 9, 17, 12.
Delayed pass to F.B. for a plunge through C. or L.G.

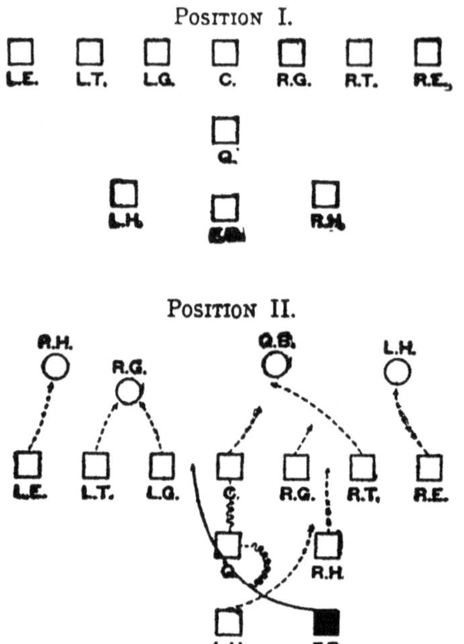

L.G. and L.T. block R.G.; C. and R.G. block opponents; L.E., R.T. and R.E. pick off secondary defense; R.H. fakes play through R.G.; L.H. follows R.H., making bluff sure; F.B. waits and after L.H. has hit line, comes across and receives ball from Q.B., who has faked a pass to R.H. and hits the line close to center; The same play may be used from a "left formation," with F.B. carrying ball through R.G.; a delayed pass in which the L.H. hits on the R.G. may be used; in this play the R.H. and F.B. cross for the L.T., then the Q.B. fakes a pass to the F.B. and after they have hit the line the L.H. crosses on the right guard.

Signal 30, as 15, 30, 12.
Quarter-back plunges through center.

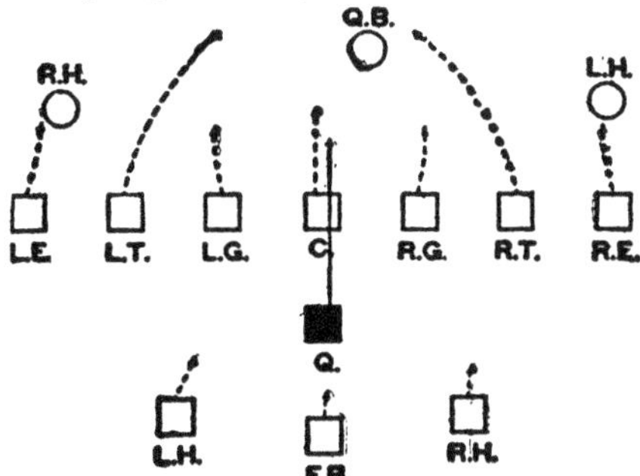

C. charges his opponents; R.G. and L.G. block opponents; L.T., R.T., L.E. and R.E. pick off secondary defense; Q.B. receives ball and follows in wake of center.

Signal 36 or 37, as 18, 36, 10.
Fake placement kick, with Q.B. carrying ball around R.E. or L.E.

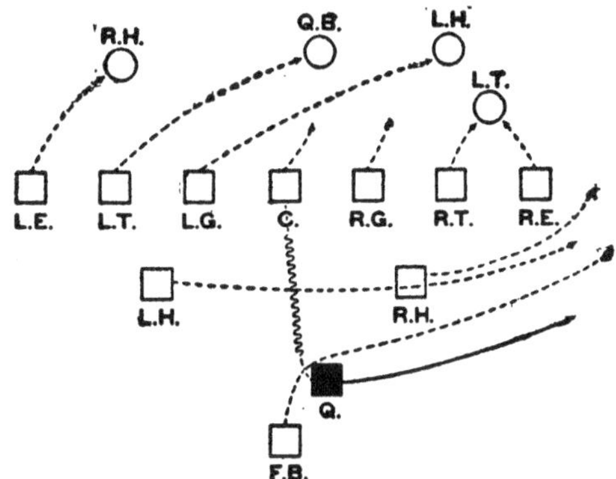

R.E. and R.T. block L.T.; R.G. and C. block opponents; L.G., L.T. and L.E. pick off secondary defense; R.H. and L.H. start for end as interference; ball passed to Q.B.; he places it on ground for kick; F.B. kicks over ball and joins interference, and Q.B. rises to feet and runs wide with ball.

Signal 22 or 23, as 15, 22, 10 to R.E. and 15, 23, 10 to L.E. Forward pass to R.E. on shift formation.

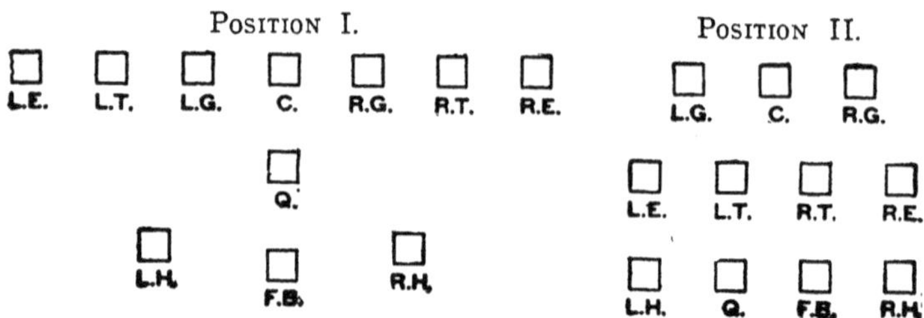

Then "shift" and

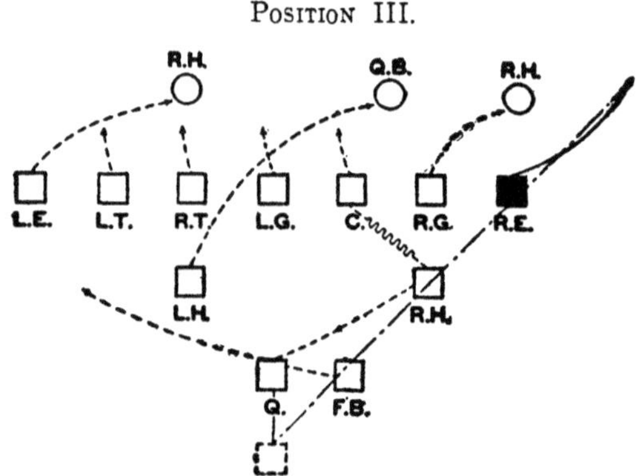

The play starts as if R.H. was carrying ball around L.E.; line charges opponents and then pick off secondary defense, after ball is caught; R.E. runs out wide; R.H. receives ball on direct pass from C. and starts as an end run; F.B. goes out to block off; L.H. cuts through line and picks off secondary defense after the pass is caught; Q.B. steps back two paces, receives ball from R.H. and makes a long pass to R.E.; the same play may be used with a shift to right and a forward pass to L.E.

Signal 28 or 29, as 15, 28, 12.
Double pass, L.H. to F.B. for a plunge through R.T.

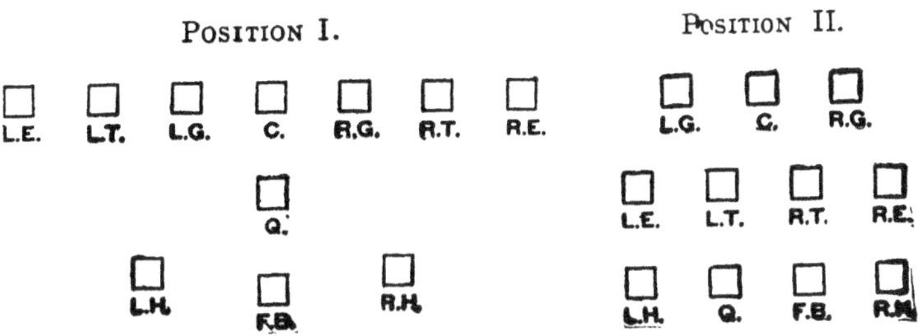

"Shift" and

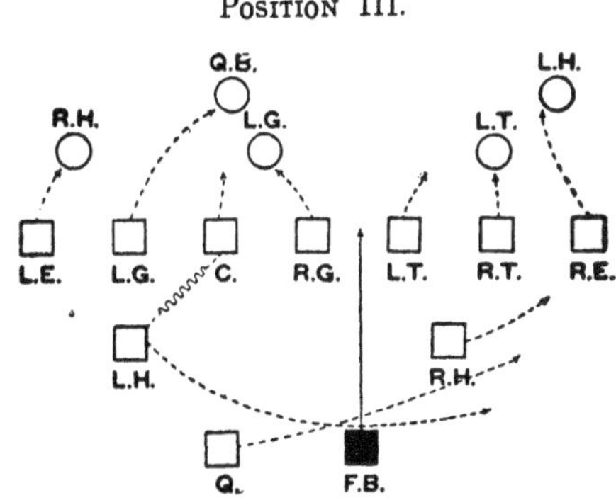

R.T. and L.T. block L.T.; R.G. and C. L.G.; R.E., L.G. and L.E. secondary defense; L.H. gets ball on direct pass and starts as on end run around R.E.; F.B. stands still and as L.H. passes him he takes the ball from him for a plunge through R.G. R.H. and Q.B. act as on run around R.E; the same play may be used with a shift to left, with Q.B. taking ball through L.G.

Signal 10, as 8, 10, 15.
Triple backward pass, with a long forward pass to Q.B.

POSITION I.

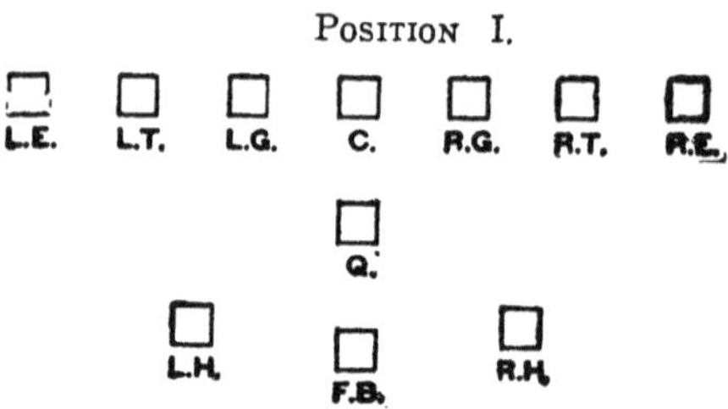

"Open formation to right" and

POSITION II.

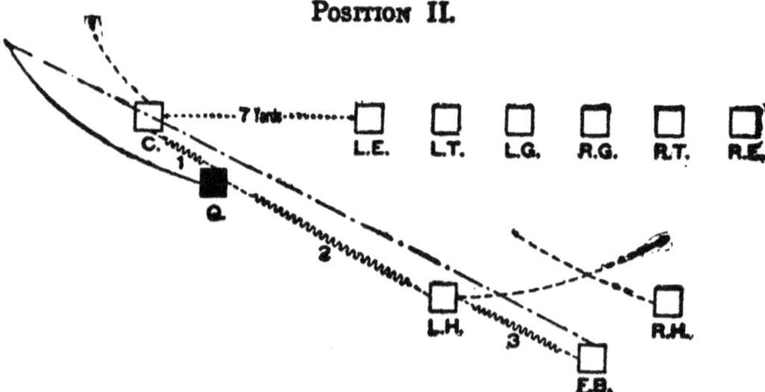

Q.B. is 2 yards in rear of center and 1½ yards to his right; L.H. in back of L.T. and 7 yards to his rear; R.H. in back of R.T. and on line with L.H.; F.B. 10 yards in rear of R.G.

Ball snapped to Q.B. who makes quick pass to L.H.; L.H. starts as if to carry ball around R.E.; F.B. starts for right side line, but halts after going three paces; R.H. crosses and protects passer; L.H. passes ball to F.B. and in the meantime Q.B. has walked out wide of all players and receives forward pass from F.B.; center picks off back-field man; line men block off opponents and after pass is caught pick off opponents.

A SEQUENCE OF PLAYS.

It frequently happens that a team, especially a school team, will have one man who has clearly outplayed every opponent he has faced and upon whom the quarter may depend when there is a distance that *must* be gained. Under such conditions a team should have a sequence of plays, i. e., three or more plays previously committed to memory, to be executed in quick succession without a signal. Assuming that the tackle is the steady and reliable man, then, select three or more plays through his position and constantly practice them as a series without any intermission.

A sequence of five plays illustrated:

Signal 5. Straight buck on L.T.
" 9. Cross-buck on L.T.
" 15. R.T. through L.T.
" 3. R.H. around L.E.
" 2. L.H. around R.E.

If the first four plays are successful the opponents will naturally shift over, to try and "brace up" the weak spot. The last play is intended to surprise them, and is therefore sent on the opposite side of the line.

The Foot Ball Code

Both in play and by tradition foot ball is a distinctively academic game—the game of the schools and the colleges. The friends of the game must accordingly rely on the schools and colleges for the preservation of its past traditions and the maintenance of the high standards of sportsmanship in its play, which are to be expected in a distinctively academic game.

In some sports it is possible to attain reasonably high standards simply by the adoption and enforcement of rules, but this is not true in foot ball. There are so many men engaged in action, the action is so rapid and so constantly shifting, that it is impossible for any official to discover every possible infraction of the rules.

There are, however, many school teams, and even some college teams, that seem to fail to recognize that the first obligation of every foot ball player is to protect the game itself, its reputation and its good name. He owes this to the game, its friends and its traditions. There can be little excuse for any college player who allows the game to be smirched with unsportsmanlike tactics.

In the case of the players in the school teams, however, unsportsmanlike play is often due largely to ignorance of what the proper standards are and what the great host of ex-foot ball players and friends of the game expect from the boys who are just learning it.

For the benefit of those who are just beginning to learn the game, the Rules Committee has decided to publish the following suggestions:

HOLDING.

Holding is prohibited by the rules because it does not belong in the game of foot ball. It is unfair play. It eliminates skill. The slowest man in the world could make a forty-yard run in every play if the rest of his teammates would hold their opponents long enough. The game is to advance the ball by strategy, skill and speed *without* holding your opponent.

Perhaps a good game could be invented, the object of which would be to advance the ball as far as possible *with* the assistance of holding your opponents, but it would not be foot ball. It would probably become a team wrestling match and, unless drastic rules rigidly enforced prevented it, a free fight. If your coach cannot show you how to gain distance without holding your opponents, get another coach. It is fair to assume that he does not understand the strategy of the game.

SIDE LINE COACHING.

Coaching from the side lines is prohibited in the rules because it is considered an unfair practice. The game is to be played by the players using their own muscle and their own brains. If an onlooker, having seen all the hands in a game of cards, undertook to tell one of the players what card to play, the other players would have just cause to object.

"BEATING THE BALL."

"Beating the ball" by an unfair use of a starting signal is nothing less than deliberately stealing an advantage from the other side. An honest starting signal is good foot ball, but a starting signal which has for its purpose starting the team a fraction of a second before the ball is put in play, in the hope that it will not be detected by the officials, is nothing short of crookedness. It is the same as if a sprinter in a hundred-yard dash had a secret arrangement with the starter to give him a tenth of a second's warning before he fired the pistol.

TALKING TO YOUR OPPONENTS.

Talking to your opponents if it falls short of being abusive or insulting is not prohibited by the rules, partly because it ought not to be necessary and partly because no rules can make a gentleman out of a mucker. No good sportsman is ever guilty of cheap talk to his opponents.

TALKING TO OFFICIALS.

When an official imposes a penalty or makes a decision he is simply doing his duty as he sees it. He is on the field representing the integrity of the game of foot ball, and his decision, even though he may have made a mistake in judgment, is final and conclusive and should be so accepted. Even if you think the decision is a mistaken one, take your medicine and do not whine about it. If there is anything to be said, let your captain do the talking. That's his business. Yours is to keep quiet and play the game.

THE FOOT BALL CODE.

You may meet players and even coaches who will tell you that it is all right to hold or otherwise violate the rules if you do not get caught. This is the code that obtains among sneak thieves and pickpockets. The crime in their code is getting caught.

The foot ball code is different. The foot ball player who intentionally violates a rule is guilty of unfair play and unsportsmanlike tactics, and whether or not he escapes being penalized, he brings discredit to the good name of the game, which it is his duty as a player to uphold.

ACCEPT NO SUBSTITUTE **THE SPALDING** (trade-mark) **TRADE-MARK** GUARANTEES QUALITY

SPALDING CORRECTLY DESIGNED FOOT BALL SHOULDER PADS

Front View of No. HYS

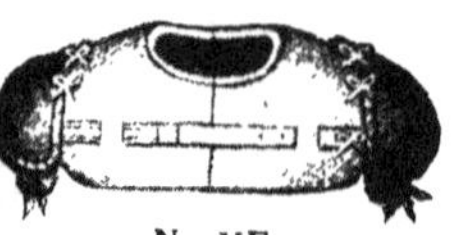
No. YF

No. **HYS.** Combined shoulder, collar bone and chest protector. Felt padded. Sole leather molded shoulder pieces, adjustable to size of player. . . . . . Each, **$5.00**

No. **YF.** Molded leather shoulder pieces, felt padded, special extra thick felt collar bone protector and adjusting straps to regulate size. Each, **$4.00** ★ *$43.20 Doz.*

No. **XF.** Combined shoulder and collarbone protector. Felt padded. Sole leather molded shoulder caps. Each, **$4.00** ★ *$43.20 Doz.*

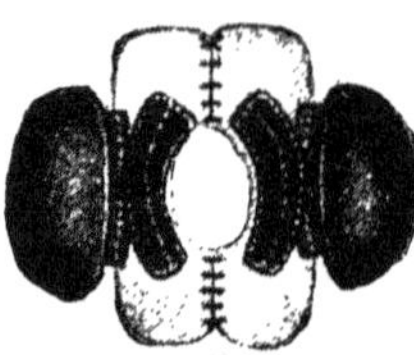
No. XF

No. XC

No. **XC.** Canvas, felt padded combined shoulder and collar bone protector. Leather covered shoulder caps. . Each, **$3.00** ★ *$32.40 Doz.*

No. **HC.** Canvas, combined shoulder and collar bone protector, fiber reinforced, padded with wool felt and canvas covered on inside. Lace adjustment. Ea., **$2.50** ★ *$27.00 Doz.*

No. **DFB.** For boys. All felt combined shoulder and collar bone protector, elastic adjustment. Each, **$1.50** ★ *$16.20 Doz.*

No. HC

No. DFB

No. **Y.** As No. YF (listed above) but without collar bone protectors. Felt padded. Fitted with adjusting straps. Special orders only. Each, **$3.00** ★ *$32.40 Doz.*

No. **MF.** As No. **YF** (listed above) but moleskin instead of leather, felt padded. Each, **$2.50** ★ *$27.00 Doz.*

No. **LL.** Large, leather, felt padded. . Each, **$2.50** ★ *$27.00 Doz.*

No. **LM.** Medium, leather, same as No. LL. Felt padded. Special order only. Ea., **$2.50** ★ *$27.00 Doz.*

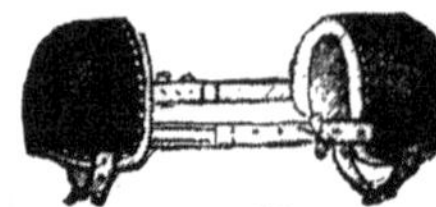
No. Y

No. LL

No. **CF.** Small, canvas, similar to No. LM. Felt padded. Each, **$1.00** ★ *$10.80 Doz.*

No. **B.** Made to fit shoulder. Heavily padded inside and out with wool felt. . . . . . . Each, **$2.50**

No. **D.** Soft black leather covering, padded with felt and fitted with adjusting lace and elastic. Selvage left for attaching. . . Each, **$1.25**

No. B

No. D

Spalding Elbow Pad

No. **EW.** Soft leather, padded with wool fleece. Pair, **$1.00**

Covered Shoulder and Elbow Pads

No. **1.** Shoulder Pad. Leather covered. Ea., **75c.** ★ *$8.10 Doz.*
No. **2.** Elbow Pad. Leather covered. " **75c.** ★ *8.10 Doz.*
No. **3.** Shoulder Pad. Canvas covered. " **30c.** ★ *3.24 Doz.*
No. **4.** Elbow Pad. Canvas covered. " **30c.** ★ *3.24 Doz.*

No. 1

No. 2

The prices printed in italics opposite ★ quoted only on orders for one-half dozen or more at one time

PROMPT ATTENTION GIVEN TO ANY COMMUNICATIONS ADDRESSED TO US | **A. G. SPALDING & BROS.** STORES IN ALL LARGE CITIES | FOR COMPLETE LIST OF STORES SEE INSIDE FRONT COVER OF THIS BOOK

PRICES SUBJECT TO CHANGE WITHOUT NOTICE. For Canadian prices see special Canadian Catalogue

FOR OUR CUSTOMERS.

THIS ORDER BLANK

IS FOR YOUR CONVENIENCE.

YOU PURCHASED THIS BOOK AT

We also sell a complete line of Spalding Athletic Goods as well as all the books of the Spalding Athletic Library.

CONSULT THE FULL LIST

FOR OTHER BOOKS ON ATHLETICS

When ordering Athletic Goods use this sheet. Simply tear it out along dotted line, fill in your wants on the reverse side, and mail it with the price as noted.

SEE THE OTHER SIDE

Gentlemen:

Enclosed please find $____________________

for which send me the articles listed below:

List Number	Quantity	Description of Article	Price

(See other side)